What people are saying about
Forgive. Freedom Is Worth It...

"I thought I understood forgiveness. I took pride in keeping short accounts with others and living unoffended. Then, I heard Laura's teaching on forgiveness and I was hit between the eyes. There were definitely people who had made my secret "list" and I had work to do with the Lord. Laura has a gift for making the principles of forgiveness applicable to each of us and helping us understand the freedom that comes with clearing our list."

—Courtney Garrett,
author of *101: Exploring The Basics of the Christian Faith*,
blogger for Sacred Story Ministries,
and Bible study teacher
Houston, Texas

"Hardly a day goes by that unforgiveness and bitterness isn't a pressing topic that comes up in my office with clients. Laura Seifert's new book will be a great source of encouragement and direction in our journey to live with emotional and relational health. Read it twice."

—Matt Barnhill M.A., CART,
director of Barnhill and Associates Counseling Centers
Houston, Texas

"Who does not want to experience true beauty from ashes? Walking through the Refiner's fire is not easy, but it's worth it. Allow Laura's honest and hilarious voice to guide you through the redemptive path to true freedom through forgiveness."

—Natalie Green,
director of strategic partnership for Africa New Life Ministries
Austin, Texas

"Not only is Laura Seifert incredibly authentic, endearing, and hilarious in this book, she clearly articulates the specific and tangible way to enjoy a life free of bitterness, envy, and despair. Her words reach us with the authority of God's Word and with the gentleness of a trusted friend. *Forgive.* is a game-changer for our soul; helping us take a hard, honest look at the one thing holding us back from a full and fruitful life. It's a must-share for your friends, co-workers, and church. I love this book. I will read it again and again."

—Kasey Van Norman,
counselor and bestselling author of *Named by God* and *Raw Faith*
College Station, Texas

"I attended one of Laura's retreats, convinced that I didn't have a problem with forgiveness. God totally laughed at that notion and set me straight that weekend. To say that I was forever changed is an understatement. Laura's book helped me dig down deep to the root of my worries, which led the Lord to give me exactly what I needed. Freedom."

—Lincee Ray,
speaker, author, and blogger of
Why I Hate Green Beans
Houston, Texas

"As you courageously enter this journey with Laura, the Holy Spirit will release a depth of insight into hidden places in your soul; places where hurts have entered your life that you may not have realized were buried deep inside you. Through laughter and tears, Laura will point you towards God's extravagant love for you, will give you some very practical tools, and you will find yourself courageously and obediently embracing the work of forgiveness. Get ready! A wellspring of refreshment will flood your soul as you release your hurts to the Lord, and you will discover a new boldness in your love for Him and for others."

—Sandy Schultz,
president and chief executive officer of The WorkFaith Connection
Houston, Texas

"A great book on forgiveness—biblical, practical, readable. It's rare when writers engage your heart with good content, reflective questions, and a dose of snarky humor. Laura relates to readers through her own stories and points you to freedom that only God can give. This is a remarkable book!"

—Sarah Harmeyer,
founder and chief people gatherer for Neighbor's Table
Dallas, Texas

"*Forgive. Freedom Is Worth It* is a must read for anyone struggling with forgiveness—which means all of us. She masterfully combines the raw, human struggle to forgive with clear, specific steps and scriptural support as to how to get there. This is one of those rare books that kept me engaged the entire way through. She allures you to the costly decision to forgive by highlighting the prize we all long for—freedom."

—Dwight Edwards,
best-selling author and founder of Revolution Within Ministries
Houston, Texas

Forgive.

FREEDOM IS WORTH IT

LAURA SEIFERT

HOUSTON, TEXAS

Forgive. Freedom Is Worth It

Published by Yes. ministries, a 501(c)(3) organization.

ISBN-13: 978-0-692-16725-0

Printed in the United States of America

Cover design by Jason Seifert
Interior formatting by Anne McLaughlin, Blue Lake Design
Author photos by Kelly Hornberger, Kelly Hornberger Photography

For Ben and Beth,
may you always run in freedom.

Contents.

Thanks.

This book is a labor of love, and it's taken a village to get here. There are so many people to thank, but let me start with my husband, Jason. You believed in me long before I believed in myself. You've prayed this book into print. Your cover design only speaks to a small part of your heart that's here. I love you and I don't deserve you.

Ben and Beth, there will never be enough words to communicate my love for you. Never. So I will continue to ask the Spirit to remind you every day. I love you more than my shoes and my jeans combined.

My family. Mommy, you've watched me grow and cheered me on every step of the way. Daddy, you'd be so proud of your girl. Kern, I pray that my son grows up to be like you. Britta, you are always grace in my life. Catherine, there's no finer woman to share a womb with and you will always be my favorite person on the planet.

Jamie, my best friend and trusted confidant.

My Board of Directors at Yes. ministries: Michelle Biggs, Sherrill Garland, Breanna Hansen, Sylvia Harris, and Nona Landers. Partnering with you in ministry has been a gift beyond measure.

Anne Finstuen, editor extraordinaire. Your passion and desire for excellence has been God honoring and butt kicking.

The incomparable, Lincee Ray. Years ago you said, "Write a book. I will help you." You've taken a massive download of words and ideas and created a structure for me to run with. Without you I'd still be staring at a blank screen with tears and snot running down my face.

Pat and Joyce Springle, you've loved the Seiferts through dark endings and bright beginnings. You've been more than mentors to

Jason and me, you're spiritual family. Thank you both for your wise counsel through this process and countless others.

Joyce Stanley, my counselor, spiritual mother, and lover of Christmas socks. Years ago, God put my hand in yours and walked me through the most life-changing journey of forgiveness. The Spirit's grace and discernment in your life led me to freedom.

And finally, all glory and honor to the One who loved me and gave Himself up for me so that I could live this truth. Jesus, You are worth it all.

Start.

I wanted to be anywhere but seated in that pleather office chair suffering and under the weight of irritatingly bad Christmas music. I wasn't really in the yuletide spirit.

It was December 2003, my husband Jason and I had just moved to our new town after he accepted a position as a worship leader for a young church. It's a long story, but all you need to know is that I wasn't happy to be there. I didn't want to move. We had only been married two years, and life was the opposite of blissful.

I left behind a community I loved, a dream role in ministry, and roots. Packing up all of our fancy china we had never used and the coffee table we bought on the side of the road for fifty dollars to start over somewhere else definitely wasn't part of my plan. Because of these and other reasons I won't bore you with, humming along to *"Jingle Bells"* in the tranquil surroundings of my therapist's office wasn't my idea of a joyful and triumphant time.

You know things are bad when Michael Bublé can't snap you out of your bah humbug mood.

To top it off, I remember glancing down and noticing that my new counselor was wearing brightly-colored Christmas socks. In that moment, it was all I could do not to get up and walk out.

What nerve. Those whimsical socks mocked me. It's like this woman was bragging, "I'm happy and you're not!" So help me if she offers me a gingerbread cookie in the shape of Rudolph. I hated everything about this place.

Then she said something that began a year-long journey that changed my life. She looked me square in the eyes and asked, "Laura, do you think you might have a problem with anger?"

Indignant, I quickly responded, "WHAT? NO!" while secretly thinking, "How dare you."

I was furious at the question. She calmly responded. "Well, I think you do. Why don't you take a week to think and pray about it and we'll pick up where we left off next week."

And that was it. She left before I did, skipping out in her snowflake socks undoubtedly headed to the mall to buy those tiny, seasonally-themed antibacterial hand sanitizers at Bath & Body Works for stocking stuffers.

I raced home with road rage like you've never seen before. Didn't she know that I was Laura Seifert? Cute, friendly, popular, and full of spunk? I'M NOT ANGRY!

Oh, but I was.

I realized over the course of that week something that I had been sensing (and ignoring) for quite some time. I wasn't myself anymore. I wasn't content. I was restless. My soul was parched and I needed something to change.

Something changed alright. Me. Forever.

My soul was parched and I needed something to change. Something changed alright. Me. Forever.

Typically, when I take a step toward God and what He wants for my life, distractions slowly begin to campaign for my attention. The second I decide to walk in obedience and faith, the attacks come from all sides. Life suddenly becomes very difficult.

There are consequences. Mistakes are made. Beliefs are compromised. Hurtful words are used. Feelings are bruised. Seeds of doubt are planted. Bitterness sets in.

One day I look up and realize I've been schlepping around a lot of unnecessary baggage. Sure, it's a matching three-piece set in pale pink with one of those nifty phone chargers built in, but that's neither here nor there. The baggage is extraneous. Although I don't need it, I choose to haul it around.

And as outrageous as it sounds, the key to lightening that load is forgiveness.

As you'll see in the pages that follow, forgiveness does not mean *sweep it under the rug... it wasn't a big deal... it didn't matter...* It does matter, so you will not be asked to gloss over painful experiences and hurtful words.

What is the state of your heart? Are you in a position to forgive old wounds or fresh offenses? When you think about the pain or emptiness you may feel, does a face come to mind? Do you see your own face? Are you ashamed to admit that God is the One you picture?

I know that making the decision to pick up this book and read its contents is a sacrifice for some of you. Instead of secretly binge watching *Friday Night Lights* (#Texasforever) on Netflix for the third time, you are reading these words.

God is going to speak to you through these pages.

This book will be worthy of your time because Scripture promises, "Come close to God, and God will come close to you" (James 4:8a), "yet He is actually not far from each of us" (Acts 17:27b ESV). It also says, "Remember, the Lord forgave you, so you must forgive others" (Colossians 3:13b).

God not only calls us to forgive, He enables us to forgive. He demonstrates forgiveness over and over and over again throughout His story. God wants to move in your life in more ways than you can imagine. And He's going to do that through the power of forgiveness.

Some of you are reading this study because of one specific need for forgiveness on your mind. It's been plaguing you and you are certain that many things will be revealed. That's great, but just be prepared for God to throw you a curveball. He's all about, *"Oh, you thought that's why you are interested in forgiveness? Ha! Good one! Buckle up. I'm about to uncover something big. Something you haven't even considered. Prepare for your mind to be blown!"*

Don't worry. That pukey sensation you're experiencing right now will eventually pass. It's a delightful mixture of fear, blended with conviction, topped off with those chili cheese fries you had for lunch. Yes, what you are feeling is extremely intimidating, but do you know what else you will feel once you push through the anxiety of the unknown?

Freedom.

You might already know that there are approximately five thousand books on the subject of forgiveness. This one isn't the final authority on the topic either. But, it is a tool that I believe the Lord wants to use in your life and mine to gain the freedom He paid for at the cross.

Take it. Read it.

Reflect on it by yourself, or explore it with a small group of friends. It's meant to encourage either or both. There are powerful truths packed in these pages. To draw closer in to the truths, you'll find a topical scripture resource in the **Notes.** It's overflowing. You may need a journal.

Pick it up. Let it be the first step in discovering the freedom God has in store for you.

I appreciate it. The Lord sees it. And you will benefit from it.

Lord, as Your beloved children, we confess that we are weary and struggling. We're running with a limp and we know that's not the way You designed it to be. Come and have Your way, Lord. Speak a word over us that jolts us with surprise. We trust You and we say thank You.

1

Favored.

"Life can only be understood backwards,
but it must be lived forwards."
Søren Kierkegaard[1]

Someone needs to cross stitch that phrase on a pillow for me. Or maybe I should tattoo it on my forehead. I want it grafted into the fibers of my being. I guarantee life would be a lot less stressful if I could just remember that hindsight is 20/20.

There are countless characters from the Old Testament who would second that emotion. If we started a Kierkegaard Club of believers, I would nominate a man named Joseph to be our chapter president. There's a passage in Genesis 50 that speaks directly to this idea.

Joseph is at the end of his life. He's surrounded by family members who deeply wounded and betrayed him. He utters this powerful thought and then dies:

"You intended to harm me, but God intended it all for good" (Genesis 50:20a).

Joseph was reminiscing. He was looking backwards as he speaks for the last time and he experiences somewhat of an "ah-ha" moment. He finally understands how it was all connected. And as

Joseph approaches the conclusion of his earthly life before he will stand before the Lord face-to-face, the curtain is peeled back and he gets it.

"They" intended to harm him. God turned that right around and used it for good. All of it.

You might be thinking that Joseph had a pretty sweet gig. You remember the headlines of his life from Sunday school and secretly wish you too had an amazing technicolor dreamcoat. His bad days weren't as bad as your bad days, right?

Wrong.

Let me tell you a little bit about Joseph's background. He was one of twelve kids and it is written in Scripture that he was the favored son. (Genesis 37:3). It was evident that his father placed him above all of his other brothers. There's a level of comfort and confidence that comes with such affirmation and Joseph walked tall in this space.

Joseph was also extremely attractive. We're talking Ryan Gosling multiplied by a thousand with a little Randall Pearson thrown in for good measure. When a man is strikingly handsome, he is distinguished from others. Women wanted to know him. Men wanted to be him.

So there's Joseph, walking around all favored and physically desirable. He was always being promoted because he was successful at everything he did. To put it bluntly, his life was moving up and to the right. He was living the American Dream.

Now, if that's all you knew about Joseph, you'd probably think he had an impressive Facebook highlight reel. With a perfect résumé like his, of course Joseph can say that God meant for his life to be good. Because on the surface, it seems like Joseph's biggest problem was dealing with all the superfluous butterflies and rainbows.

Seriously. I'd like to know how "they" intended to harm him. Was it a bad haircut that threatened Joseph's social status? Did his diamond sandals produce blisters? Could mom and dad only afford one camel on his sixteenth birthday?

In our Western culture, to be blessed means that we have Joseph's kind of Facebook life. Thanks to social media, we often choose to post our happy high points. I know I only share precious pictures of myself. If my chins make an appearance, I'm out. I'm not posting it. And I will unfriend you socially and in real life if you tag me on anything that is less than adorable.

Filters are our lifeblood, people. Use them.

Let's get back to Joseph. I want to fill in the blanks of this seemingly perfect guy's highlight reel. We're going to step into Joseph's timeline and explore what it might have been like to live in his trenches.

We know that he was one of twelve siblings and he was the favorite. The problem is that Joseph's brothers hated him for it and that made his home life extremely hard. Raise your hand if you can relate to colorful family dynamics!

When Joseph was seventeen-years-old, he had a dream. This means that teenage Joseph had an encounter with God that marked him for life. Although this was a holy moment, our Abercrombie model didn't soar after his vision. It took one foolish mistake for our boy to crash and burn. Here's what happened:

> One night Joseph had a dream, and when he told his brothers about it, they hated him more than ever. "Listen to this dream," he said. "We were out in the field, tying up bundles of grain. Suddenly my bundle stood up, and your bundles all gathered around and bowed low before mine!" His brothers responded, "So you think you will be our king, do you? Do you actually think you will reign over us?" And they hated him all the more because of his dreams and the way he talked about them (Genesis 37:5-8).

Be honest. You can see why Joseph's brothers were annoyed, right? I'm not sure if Joseph reported the dream with an arrogant tone, but the fact remains that neither Joseph nor his brothers understood the meaning of the vision. Was it a smart decision for Joseph to blab specific details? I'll give him a pass on this one. He was just a kid excited to share his encounter with God with his family. Was it appropriate for the brothers to act like punks and openly hate him for it? Certainly not. The story continues:

> Soon Joseph had another dream, and again he told his brothers about it. "Listen, I have had another dream," he said. "The sun, moon, and eleven stars bowed low before me!" This time he told the dream to his father as well as to his brothers, but his father scolded him. "What kind of dream is that?" he asked. "Will your mother and I and your brothers actually come and bow to the ground before you?" But while his brothers were jealous of Joseph, his father wondered what the dreams meant (Genesis 37:9-11).

Okay, this time I can't defend Joseph. Did he learn nothing from his family's reaction to the first dream? What was he thinking? This is when Joseph's Instagram profile begins to paint a different picture than what we know to be true.

Did he learn nothing from his family's reaction to the first dream? What was he thinking?

The brothers are so livid with Joseph's arrogant behavior that they literally plot to kill him. Judah steps in and suggests that instead of taking their younger brother's life, why not make a little change and sell him as a slave to a band of Egyptians?

Well, this is a dip in the timeline. Joseph has been betrayed by people he should have been able to trust. Even the Valencia filter can't help this situation.

The good news is that Joseph was sold to a key Egyptian leader named Potiphar. He puts Joseph as second in command and just like that, our dreamer suddenly has power and favor again. Let's post a new update folks! Things are looking good.

When Joseph settles into his new role, celebrating a life that is moving up and to the right, Potiphar's wife enters the picture. She was drawn to handsome Joseph like any human being with functioning eyeballs. Here's the problem: Not only was she married to Joseph's boss, but she is used to getting whatever she wants. And she wants Joseph.

But Joseph is a man of integrity and he denies all of her advances. As a result, Potiphar's wife accuses Joseph of rape and has him thrown in prison. So much for good times.

After spending some time in jail, Joseph is favored again by Pharoah, who is Egypt's king. Pharaoh puts Joseph in charge and he saves an entire nation (and the family who betrayed him) from famine. Joseph is once again very powerful.

He's always been favored. This time, he has purpose.

Engage.

When was the first time you had a sense that God really saw you?

Think of a moment in your life when you made a mistake and wanted to take it back. (Buying those ugly shoes that one time does not count!)

Have you ever been betrayed by people you trusted? How did it make you feel? Did you reconcile the relationship? If not, what is keeping you from reaching out to make amends?

Read Romans 12:14-21. How would your life be different if you could fully live out this passage?

Jesus, You bless me with such encouragement on this journey of forgiveness. You are my helper and I will have no fear. Speak to me about my life. Enlighten me. Show me what I need to know about You and about me in this process. I trust You.

2

Stuck.

Whether you are basking in your own highs or enduring your own lows right now, most all of us suffer from an identity crisis at some point in time. We play the comparison game and long for the attributes we see in others. We want the beefy financial account of our neighbors down the street. We crave a fulfilling career. We wish we could have the fabulous metabolism of the woman at the gym, who also never seems tired. We covet a healthy marriage like all of our friends have, or a house full of kids. We dream of the days we were wrinkle free, cellulite free, and worry free.

We have a tendency to compare our weaknesses, or perceived weaknesses, with the strengths of others. We do the same with our wants, our needs, and our desires. And guess what? We are rarely satisfied when we engage in this silly pastime.

I had great parents who loved me. That was a high on my timeline. But they got divorced when I was a young girl. That was a gut punch. Thankfully, I began to grow in my relationship with the Lord and I remember His comfort. It was a powerful feeling. Big high. Then I kissed a lot of boys and that didn't lead me in a good direction. Major low.

I lived at happy hour as often as I could for a few years. Then I came back to the Lord and got connected to a good church. When

I met Jason, I was up in airplane altitude. I unexpectedly plunged into a free fall during our first year of marriage. No one told me how hard it would be to share my life with someone else.

We sought wisdom from gifted counselors and learned how to navigate our partnership. But then I got into ministry and encountered major wounds from the job I thought I always wanted. Low, low, low.

Have you ever met anyone who pulled a Joseph and declared, "Oh my goodness, you meant that for harm. You meant to puncture me and hurt me. Nevertheless, I see what God was doing. It was all for good. No worries."

For most of us, we don't see ourselves at the end of our lives uttering those words. Let me be clear, it's not because God isn't present. It's not because God doesn't want to turn it around. It's not because God doesn't love you. It's not because God doesn't long for a relationship with you. It's not because God has forgotten you.

We need to rejoice in the fact that we are all created in the image of God. John 3:16 says, "For God loved the world so much that He gave His one and only Son, so that everyone who believes in Him will not perish but have eternal life."

I need to rest in that truth. Especially when the pitfalls start to add up. You see, the dark moments are like adhesive that clings to my skin. So much so that it literally makes me stuck.

Once upon a time, I was cute. I had a ton of friends and lived it up, but part of the reason I dated so many boys was because I had daddy issues that stemmed from my parents' divorce.

By the grace of God, I married a great man. Truly. Anyone will tell you that I married up. But if that is the case, then why was my marriage so hard year one?

It was the adhesive. All of the dark stuff was clinging to me. And since I didn't know how to deal with the stickiness or how to forgive the person who contributed to my stuck state, I stuffed my emotions way, way down.

The Scriptures tell us in Hebrews that there is a race that has been set before us. (Hebrews 12:1). There is a call on your life that's going to lead you. It's going to provide joy and intimacy with the Lord and the greatest sense of purpose in your life.

Unfortunately, no matter what my sixth grade teacher Miss Stubblefield told me, I am not perfect. No one is perfect. Life is full of amazing moments, but it's also full of unexpected twists and turns. There are wounds that come into our lives, disappointments, or dreams that aren't fulfilled. There are desires that you still long for. There are rejections that you've received from loved ones.

We live in a sinful world and the enemy is prowling around like a lion, just waiting for an opportunity to intervene in our lives. He wants us to trip up on a million tiny distractions. Do you know why?

Because you cannot run when you are entangled.

So what are we supposed to do? How do we get unstuck? Is there a pill we can take or a high impact workout routine that can do the trick? If we purchase enough Diet Cokes from Sonic with the good crushed ice, will that give us the energy to stave off the darkness?

I wish.

Scripture offers a suggestion. We're told to throw it off.

Don't you love it when the Bible is nice and vague? What does that even mean? Are we just supposed to think positive thoughts and wish it away? Should we try and take care of it ourselves? If it is in our benefit to run this race, yet we know there will be roadblocks and challenges along the way, shouldn't there be an easy recipe for success?

We're in luck! There is a straightforward answer and no, it is not served in a Route 44-sized cup. The very next verse points the way. "And let us run with perseverance the race marked out for us, fixing our eyes on Jesus, the pioneer and perfecter of faith" (Hebrews 12:1b-2a NIV).

The answer is Jesus. He removes all of the sticky entanglements. He is the One who can help us run the race and run it well.

The answer is Jesus. He removes all of the sticky entanglements. He is the One who can help us run the race and run it well. And He does this through our capacity to forgive.

Some of you have been stuck for a very long time. If you die tomorrow, you know that by grace through faith, you will go to heaven because you believe that Jesus is your Lord and Savior. That's a wonderful reality and I'm thrilled you have reached that decision.

But what will your disposition be when you get to heaven? Will you have a full heart like Joseph? Or will it be hardened and calloused?

God continues to free my paralyzed heart year after year. My prayer is that He molds me to be more like Joseph. I want to look back at the end of my life and rejoice. I'm willing to do the work. The work of forgiveness. It's definitely a refining process and don't for one second think it will be easy.

Just know it will be worth it.

"It is for freedom that Christ has set us free" (Galatians 5:1a NIV). Listen, do not let yourself be bound by another yoke of slavery. Life is messy. It's hard and I sometimes feel like it's getting darker by the minute. You're not going to reach the other side unscathed. That's a huge bummer, I know.

Try focusing on the fact that you won't be enslaved if you forgive. Your battle scars can have a beautiful healing over them if you let Jesus do His work in your life.

Joseph allowed the Lord to do just that when he centered his entire being around four truths:

- God is in control.
- God is good.
- God is always present.
- God is always at work.

Maybe you think that because of a foolish mistake, the presence of God has left you. Maybe you think because of so many wounds that you've experienced, you're not willing to open up and trust again.

Those thoughts are invalid.

God is pursuing you. God loves you and Jesus died for you so that you could run with freedom. It's not just about getting into heaven in the future. It's about living right now full of joy and peace.

God is pursuing you. God loves you and Jesus died for you so that you could run with freedom. It's about living right now full of joy and peace.

So many of us boldly proclaim, "I'm going to receive Jesus' forgiveness for my sins and invite Him into my life and now I'm going to heaven. From that point forward, I'm just going to white knuckle it and do the best I can to be a good person until I get there."

That's what I did, at least. It lasted about thirty minutes.

I came to the place where I could not pretend anymore. I was in full-time ministry and I was so tired of having it all together. I was weary of going to church every weekend, leading Bible studies, and I could not stand before a crowd and declare, "God is so good!"

I knew that sentiment was the "right" thing to say, but I didn't believe it in my gut. My life was a complicated labyrinth of twisted up knots. Thankfully, the Lord in His grace started to untangle each one bit by bit.

He can do that for you, too. He wants to do that for you. Because He favors you. Read these words in Zephaniah 3:17 and let them sink into your bones:

> For the Lord your God is living among you.
> He is a mighty Savior.
> He will take delight in you with gladness.
> With His love, He will calm all your fears.
> He will rejoice over you with joyful songs.

For some, that makes us uncomfortable. There's an underlying twinge of "yeah, right" when we contemplate the meaning of these verses. We feel we haven't earned the right to be rejoiced over with joyful songs.

Consider this: Is there any part of the passage that states you deserve the Lord delighting and rejoicing in you? Read carefully. Does it?

No.

He delights in us and rejoices over us because He loves us.

Engage.

Have you ever felt like your past has haunted you? Was there ever an instance when you thought you escaped a period of time in your life and suddenly it popped up again?

Do you remember the first time you were rejected? Did you feel at a loss on how to fix the situation?

Can you identify the sticky points that are currently weighing you down?

Do you have the courage to ask the Lord to reveal places in your life where you may be stuck?

Lord, for those of us who have been in the darkness for a long time, I pray that Your joy begins to break through. Thank You for being faithful. Help us to step off our performance treadmills of trying to make ourselves worthy of Your favor and allow us to receive the truth—that You delight in us and long to sing over us.

3

Tangled.

Jason and I got married in October 2001. Have I mentioned that I married up? I did. He's the best man I could ever ask for. He's kind, generous, funny, and deeply devoted to Jesus.

But he's still a man.

He's not perfect. There are many times I've said to him, "You're lucky you're funny" or "It's a good thing you're cute." Marriage is not for the faint of heart. Becoming one flesh as scripture tells us in Genesis 2:24, ain't easy. Our first year of marriage seemed more like a war zone instead of a love nest. It seemed like we fought about everything.

I remember one of our biggest arguments happened over a coffee pot. That's right, a coffee pot. How insane is that? He thought it should be black and I thought it obviously needed to be white to match the rest of the appliances.

You know I'm right, people.

We argued about the shower curtain being closed or open when we weren't using it. (PS: The correct answer is closed.) Fortunately the tie that bound us together was the fact that we didn't argue over the toilet paper roll being pulled from the top or bottom. And if I have to tell you the right way, you need professional help. There's only one way to pull the toilet paper from the roll. One. Way.

If I had to name or describe my first year of marriage, one phrase comes to mind—turf wars. Without consciously realizing it, we were in an all out battle for control. And that battle was fueled from a place of fear that had developed over the years. Fear crept into our lives because we both encountered wounds as children. We all do. I have a jar on my kitchen counter that you might mistake for a tip jar, but in fact it's there to pay for the counseling my kids will need as they grow up in my house. Parents are human, too.

Within six short months of "wedded bliss," I distinctly remember laying in bed one night with Jason. We were both silent, staring at the ceiling. Looking up with eyes full of anguish, Jason said, "Marriage is so hard."

If we were truly honest, we would both admit to wondering if we'd made a mistake by getting married in the first place. We followed all of the right steps. We dated for more than a year. Friends who witnessed our relationship rooted for us. We sought premarital counseling from a trusted pastor who gave us a green light to move forward. All compatibility tests were passed with flying colors. We were set up for success.

So why was this marriage thing such a struggle?

Jason and I found ourselves seated in a counselor's chair soon after we said "I do." We weren't equipped to navigate turf wars on our own. I believe it was within the safe context of a covenant that God wanted to start uncovering the things that weighed us down.

What we believed to be the problem (each other) really wasn't the problem at all. We walked into this union with a truckload of baggage that had accumulated from years of unresolved pain. Each suitcase was neatly packed with wounds, disappointment, rejection, self protection, and more wounds. Those suitcases began to serve as both weapons and barricades, blocking the intimacy God designed for our marriage to provide.

In order for us to last thirty minutes, much less thirty years, the baggage had to go. The wounds Jason and I had never dealt with were keeping us from running freely. We were tangled up.

This is true for everybody. As we run our race, we unknowingly pick up things along the way that weigh us down. What's interesting is that as we're running, we don't even really realize they are there.

Hebrews 12:1(NIV) says, "Therefore, since we are surrounded by such a great cloud of witnesses, let us throw off everything that hinders and the sin that so easily entangles. And let us run with perseverance the race marked out for us."

Before we dive into the things that hinder and the sin that entangles us (fun topic!), let's talk about this huge cloud of witnesses. Who are these people? Do we all have one of those clouds following us around?

Great question. The witnesses are men and women who have gone before us in the faith. They are the Josephs of the world who remind us, "He is worth it. God is worth it. Keep going. Don't give up. Don't let these things take you out of the race."

The author of Hebrews wants you to know that this can be done. It is possible to "throw off" all the weight that slows us up. Especially the sin that "so easily entangles" our progress. We will be able to run with endurance the race that God has set out before us.

All we have to do is keep our eyes on Jesus.

You see, the enemy loves for us to glance at someone else's race. We check out her Facebook highlight reel and mistakenly conclude that her life is a dream. She's always beautiful. She can buy anything she wants. Her marriage is thriving. She appears to have it all.

Suddenly, we're wishing for her life. A life that we assume has zero valleys, zero sticky points, and zero problems. We fall into the trap of adopting an unhealthy expectation that a successful life is equivalent to continued peaks in our timeline. Therefore, valleys must be a sign of failure and defeat.

Did that last sentence resonate with you? Are you a little twitchy that I labeled all valleys as a colossal disappointment on your part?

Well, it's true. Valleys can be a consequence, better known as really stupid choices we made in our past. Or they can depict a time when someone else damaged our hearts and lost our trust completely.

Valleys can be a consequence, better known as really stupid choices we made in our past. Or they can depict a time when someone else damaged our hearts and lost our trust completely.

Do you see the difference? In one instance, we made a willing choice. In the other, we were the recipient of pain.

We see this in Joseph's life. He was an arrogant teenager who made the conscious decision to tell everyone at the breakfast table leaning over their bowls of Cheerios, "Hey, you're going to bow down to me one day!"

That was Joseph's choice. But then his brothers took it a step further by plotting to kill him and selling him into slavery. That was not Joseph's choice.

There is pressure in this day and age to thrive. I must find the right skin product so my neck never sags. I must have a picturesque family picture on our Christmas cards. Should we wear white linen outfits on the beach? Or is it a simple theme this year with a rustic barn and a rented golden retriever?

We presume success has a formula. By age twenty-three, I'll be married to Tim Riggins. He will coach football for a living and I will be a successful lawyer and the youngest partner at the firm by age thirty. At thirty-two, I will walk away from my career to raise our three children. The little darlings will not be hoodlums and will flourish under my tutelage to be upstanding citizens of this world. Tim and I will grow old together and look forward to rocking countless grandbabies on the front porch of my dream home that Tim built with his own two muscular hands.

Clear eyes. Full hearts. Can't lose.[2]

In reality, there are two possible scenarios for this situation. Either it never happens and you are disappointed that your life isn't moving up and to the right, or it does happen and it's not quite how you anticipated your personal paradise to feel. We make choices. People make choices for us. Pain inevitably makes an appearance and we're shocked because on top of that pain is a layer of shame.

We make choices. People make choices for us. Pain inevitably makes an appearance and we're shocked because on top of that pain is a layer of shame.

I should have known better.
I should have been able to do better.
I should have figured that out.
This should not have happened.

Jason and I went to Israel in 2013. In the city of Jerusalem, there's an area of the Temple Mount called the Wailing Wall. Hundreds of people visit every day to write down a heartfelt prayer and wedge it between the bricks. Everywhere you look, someone is huddled over a tiny scrap of paper or vying for a spot near the wall. Reading the faces of those composing earnest requests, it's easy to tell who is aching, who needs fixing, who longs for a change.

One thing I found very interesting is that the wall is segregated. Men have a huge chunk of the wall, while the women have just a sliver. The day I visited, there were triple the amount of women in the section that had been allotted to us and barely any on the men's side. Ladies were literally standing up on chairs. I saw them on each other's shoulders. They were broken. They were crying out. They were desperate to have their prayers heard.

My heart went out to all of them. For many reasons.

There is a belief system at play that God is going to really pay special attention to these particular prayers if you can manage to draft your request respectfully and gently force your way to the wall to locate a home for your piece of paper.

I remember at the time, my daughter Beth was scheduled to have open heart surgery later that year and I was a hot mess. I didn't want to see my baby girl prepped with needles and rolled off behind two sterile double doors in a cold hospital. I didn't want to trust her little body and her vulnerable heart with a doctor and a team of nurses.

I dug through my bag and ripped off the corner from day one of our trip itinerary. I searched frantically for a pen and miraculously found one amidst the half eaten Kind bar, Ziploc baggie of Advil, a bottle of sunscreen, and loose shekels.

Snacks, ibuprofen, SPF 50, and money for souvenirs. That's all you need for a trip to the Holy Land. You're welcome.

Standing near that wall, I wrote five words down on my janky piece of paper stained with backpack residue. I vowed that I would climb the shoulders of a stranger to shove my wish into the crevices of that wall. Because my message was more important than the others.

"Lord, would You heal Beth?"

Engage.

Read Hebrews 12:1-3. Do you have a personal cloud of witnesses who have gone before you? Write down their names and remember how their lives impacted you for good.

Do you believe fixing your eyes on Jesus results in not growing weary or losing heart? What do these verses tell you? How do you fix your eyes on Jesus?

What are some of the ways you feel pressure to thrive in your day-to-day routine?

What would you write on a scrap of paper if you were standing in front of the Wailing Wall right now?

Lord, You are God that frees me. You are God that makes me run freely. By Your grace, would You show me where I'm tangled? And would You be merciful to extend the courage I need to throw off the baggage You reveal?

4

Wounded.

I once had a vivid dream that I was walking down a hospital hallway. I saw four girls and one was on the ground holding her mangled leg. The weird part is that her friends were just talking as the girl sat there with a bloody, hemorrhaging appendage.

I remember thinking, "No. This is not okay. She must get well." I was a little disappointed that Dream Laura didn't have a doctorate in medicine. I guess my brain is incapable of math and science in both the real world and in dreamland. Shocker. I put the girl on a gurney and led her to the professionals who could mend her leg.

When I woke up, I sensed God unpacking my dream for me. The girls were sitting in a hospital. We are sitting in a church.

Oftentimes, we walk into the sanctuary damaged. Even though we are surrounded by our friends and family, they have all become so accustomed to our limps and wounds, that we no longer really see them. We hold our wounds because they hurt, but everyone around us sits in the same place and acts like it's normal.

Because it is normal. Living with the pain is our new normal.

We can go to happy hour repeatedly every Thursday and we can gripe about our lacerated leg. We can talk about it all day long to the point that it becomes a part of who we are and what we do. We start to lose sight that anything will change. We don't even pray that it's going to change.

All of a sudden, someone recognizes that we are not okay. And they offer to take us to get help, because they know they don't have the capabilities to do it themselves. They offer to take us to the Healer.

"I can't heal you. But I know Who can."

Beth had a hole in her heart and there was a surgeon who cut her open and fixed it. I don't know how he did it. I don't need to know the details of how he did it.

I just know that she's well, and that's good enough for me.

I don't pretend to understand how Jesus is going to fix your wounds. That's not for me to know. My little head can't figure it all out, and that's fine because I'm not responsible for you. I'm not responsible for my kids. I'm not responsible for my husband. I'm not responsible for my sister. Those that I love the dearest, I'm still not responsible for them. As my friend and mentor Matt Barnhill says, "I'm not responsible ***for*** them, but I am responsible ***to*** them."

My job is simple. All I have to do is take the wounded to the Healer.

My job is simple. All I have to do is take the wounded to the Healer.

God forbid if I refuse to do that because I'm nervous that it may seem awkward.

God forbid that I would sit there on a church floor or a hospital floor when my friend is hemorrhaging and suggest, "Hey girl, patch it up a little bit. It's not going to hurt as much if you bandage it. Here's a princess Band-Aid. That should make you feel better. Another round of margaritas for the bleeder over here, please!"

There's a story in the Gospel of Mark that illustrates this idea perfectly.

> When Jesus returned to Capernaum several days later, the news spread quickly that He was back home. Soon the house where He was staying was so packed with visitors that there was no more room, even outside the door. While He was preaching God's word to them, four men arrived carrying a paralyzed man on a mat. They couldn't bring him to Jesus because of the crowd, so they dug a hole through the roof above His head. Then they lowered the man on his mat, right down in front of Jesus (Mark 2:1-4).

First of all, let's give the paralyzed guy a name. I'm going to call him Johnny Castle. Secondly, I absolutely love that his friends ripped a hole in the roof of some stranger's house to lower their friend down to Jesus. Something tells me these guys have a membership to the Capernaum CrossFit gym.

Johnny can't walk and his friends have heard enough about Jesus to believe He can help. They don't know what's going to happen. They don't know what Jesus will do. They don't know what He might say. But they can carry Johnny to the Healer. Whatever it takes is what they will do.

So that's what they did.

You need these types of friends in your life. You don't need a group who are going to fix you. You need a group who will be honest enough to say, "I think you are wounded. I see you. Let me pray for you. Let me point you to Jesus. Let me take you to Him."

That's what these sweet friends did for Johnny. They lowered him down right to the feet of Jesus. They knew if they could just get in front of Him, He would answer their prayers the way they wanted them answered.

The story continues in verse 5, "Seeing their faith, Jesus said to the paralyzed man, 'My child, your sins are forgiven.'"

Stop. Take that in for just a second.

Jesus called him "my child." This is a grown man. Jesus didn't say, "Hey, Johnny" or "Hey, dude." He said, "My child, your sins are forgiven."

What had that man done to earn that title?

Nothing.

If you're like me, you blaze right through the "my child" business and zero in on the "you are forgiven" part. As a friend peering down at Jesus through an opening from a thatched roof I just ruined on purpose, I'm the one interjecting my irritation regarding what just went down.

"Excuse me, Jesus, but we are sooooo glad you forgave Johnny, but what we really need is healing. That's why we took the time to carry him across town, up a ladder, and down through a hole in this roof. His sins are forgiven. That's fabulous. Now what about that paralysis part? We'd like him to walk again, please and thank you."

Yeah. I'm the one telling Jesus how I would prefer for Him to answer my prayers. I'm sure He finds that delightful.

Has anybody else been there? Have you found yourself arguing with the Lord that He isn't fixing the prayer you took the time to write down and stuff into the Wailing Wall? How presumptuous of Him. Clearly you know what's best. The solution is obvious, isn't it? Quick, easy answers in a timely manner are preferred. Hop to it, Jesus.

How many of you have come to the Lord with a certain need only to discover that He's working in your heart to get to the core of another matter? How aggravating is that? You're minding the gap between your wounded friend and the Healer and He has the gall to gut check you while you're interceding for someone else? What's up with that, Jesus?

Let's look at it from a different perspective. Why do you think Jesus told Johnny that his sins were forgiven? Why didn't He heal him, suggest he start going by the more professional name of John, and then tell him his sins were forgiven?

Jesus could heal Johnny in the blink of an eye, but if Johnny's sins were not forgiven, he was spiritually dying. Jesus knew that Johnny's greatest need, above and beyond the physical act of walking, was his need to be forgiven and reconciled with God.

Jesus did not come to make bad people good. He came to make dead people alive.

When we are living our life apart from forgiveness, we are dying. Jesus knew that, and Jesus said, "My child." He may be speaking directly to Johnny, but Jesus is also communicating to the men and women who are packed into that house listening to every word and watching His every step. Jesus wants the audience to understand that He is moving toward this person, His child, in love.

Jesus did not come to make bad people good. He came to make dead people alive.

And the most loving thing Jesus can do is forgive us. All of us.

The passage goes on to say that the teachers of the law thought this act of forgiveness was blasphemy. Only God can forgive. Jesus knew what they were thinking, so He poses a question.

> But some of the teachers of religious law who were sitting there thought to themselves, "What is he saying? This is blasphemy! Only God can forgive sins!"

> Jesus knew immediately what they were thinking, so he asked them, "Why do you question this in your hearts? Is it easier to say to the paralyzed man 'Your sins are forgiven,' or 'Stand up, pick up your mat, and walk'? So I will prove to you that the Son of Man has the authority on earth to forgive sins." Then Jesus turned to the paralyzed man and said, "Stand up, pick up your mat, and go home!"
>
> And the man jumped up, grabbed his mat, and walked out through the stunned onlookers (Mark 2:6-12a).

I like to think the first thing Johnny did with his brand new legs after high fiving his roof buddies was run to Kellerman's so he could share the last dance with Baby. I bet he had the time of his life.

Healing Johnny immediately would have been really cool. Folks would have traveled around following Jesus to see what He would do next, I'm sure. He could have been a player in *The Greatest Showman* standing beside the bearded lady claiming, "This is me!"

But that would not have brought those men and women to their knees in worship. That would not have caused the witnesses to say, "You are my Savior. You are the Messiah. You are Yeshua. I need you."

What Jesus is teaching us is that healing someone is easier than forgiving someone.

Why is it so difficult to forgive sin? Because there's always a cost.

Why is it so difficult to forgive sin? Because there's always a cost. In the Old Testament, anytime sin occurred, there had to be a payment for it. And the payment had to be alive, seeing that the wages of sin is death.

Back then, people had to track down an unadulterated, spotless animal. Whether it was a lamb, or a goat, or a heifer, it had to be pure and it had to be killed. In order to atone, or to cover your sin, there had to be a substitution.

Think about a substitute teacher. That person is filling in because the real teacher can't be in class. Substitutionary atonement is a big churchy word that means someone has to pay for my sin, because it's not going to be me.

When Jesus tells Johnny, "Your sins are forgiven," the teachers of the law understand the Old Testament ways and they can't compute. They know God is the only One who can forgive and there has to be blood. The sin has to be covered. Something has to die in your place.

John 1:29 affirms that Jesus is the Lamb of God. He would be the final substitute.

God is pure, spotless, and holy. I'm tainted with sin, which makes me unholy. My unholiness cannot intermingle with His holiness. My sins cut me off from God. (Isaiah 59:2).

When I'm cut off from God, I'm separated from Him. The good news is that God wants me back. And He wanted Johnny back into relationship with Him. By forgiving this man's sin, He restored his relationship with God.

Engage.

Do you identify with the girl who is holding her wounded leg? Is there pain that runs so deep, you've just learned to live with it?

Is there a Johnny in your life who needs to be carried to Jesus? If so, will you commit to having an awkward conversation with that person?

When is the last time you thought of yourself as God's child? What other ways would He describe you?

Spend a few minutes reflecting on the fact that God sent His Son to atone for your sins.

Jesus, You love me. I want to know that in my gut. Thank You for loving me even when I don't completely grasp or feel that love. And when I'm broken, thank You for being the only source for healing. Move me closer to wholeness in You. There's no other way but You.

5

Messy.

Let's talk about sin.

I know. Not your average icebreaker. But we need to understand the mechanics of sin before we can move on to the forgiveness part.

We often think of sin as "bad deeds." Although that is a true assessment, it's much more complicated.

In my mind, I see sin as a dividing wall. It's a condition I'm born into, thanks Adam and Eve. (Genesis 3, Ephesians 2:1). It keeps me from God.

Remember, I'm tainted with sin, which makes me unholy.

It separates me from the intimate relationship for which I was designed. What's even more concerning is that I can't remove this obstruction on my own.

Scripture says in Isaiah 59:2, "It's your sins that have cut you off from God. Because of your sins, He has turned away and will not listen anymore."

Because of my sins, I laid the brickwork that alienates me from my Lord. Sin by sin, brick by brick, I constructed this barrier. As a result, I go through life managing this blockade, constantly frustrated because I have no idea how to knock it down. I try my hardest to get to God on the other side, but I just can't.

I try to connect with Him.
I try to understand Him.
I try to see Him.
I try to please Him.
I try to break through.
Nothing works.

As a result, I take matters into my own hands. I proudly proclaim that I will fix the problem and step one is figuring out what God wants from me. I make a game plan and vow to be super nice. To everyone. Even my evil officemate. Kindness will definitely weaken the structure. Then I'll be united with God.

Next, I declare that I'm going to stop doing all the bad stuff. I'll no longer hang out with unfavorable influences. Following that, I continue making good choices by giving to a reputable cause. I write a big fat check to the organization and post about it on Facebook so everyone else will know how generous I am.

Finally, I collect flip flops to mail to poor kids in Africa. As an added bonus, I promise to serve at a soup kitchen on Thanksgiving. Better yet, I'll devote my beloved Christmas morning to serving the homeless. If it's bad weather, I won't stay long, but I'll still go.

Surely that will be enough to tear down the wall, right?

Wrong. All of these solutions fall short. Eventually, the vein in my forehead will pop and I won't be nice to that belligerent coworker because she threw me under the bus at a meeting. I'll stop writing checks to nonprofits and sending flip flops because I have to pay the credit card bill and I'll skip out on serving at the soup kitchen because I've got a thousand items on my to-do list that must be completed by the end of the week.

Furthermore, the coworker doesn't deserve kindness, other people can write checks and send flip flops, and the soup kitchen will be there next week.

The excuses weigh me down and I feel like there's something entangling me. I can't run. Something isn't right. Things don't make sense.

The next natural thing to do is compare myself to other people. I see the freedom in my friend's eyes and how she worships the Lord and I secretly chastise myself because I can't connect that way. She must pray every morning, serve all the livelong day, and constantly read her Bible. Clearly there's something she's doing right that I haven't tapped into yet.

Sound familiar?

We compare ourselves to others over and over again. Sadly, we remain in a cycle of defeat because our best works get us nowhere. We can't remove the wall of sin ourselves. Our good deeds won't do it. Our morality won't do it. There's only one solution.

Jesus, the pure, spotless Lamb of God.

In Ezekiel 36:26, the Sovereign Lord says, "And I will give you a new heart, and I will put a new spirit in you. I will take out your stony, stubborn heart and give you a tender, responsive heart." In other words, "I'm going to remove this dividing wall, and I'm going to replace it with a soft, malleable heart."

How does He do that?

By taking on the sins of the entire world and dying on a cross so we can be forgiven and, in response, learn to forgive.

If you were to stand before the Lord right now, do you think He is concerned with your good deeds? How many people you served?

The dollar amount from the money you gave? All of the hours you spent in the church nursery? Memorizing Romans 12?

Okay, Cindi, let's watch the highlight reel of your life. There's that time you tried to be nice, oh and there's that meal you served the elderly man. Good, good. I see you were a foster parent. Awesome. Oh wait! You only fed that man once. And there you are yelling at that foster kid. Dang. Now what are we going to do? Let's tally up your scoresheet and see what happens.

Do you really think the good outweighing the bad is going to be your golden ticket? If the scales tip in the right direction, you'll instantaneously get your complimentary punch card to Heavenly Starbucks?

Of course not. You can't earn salvation. It is ours by grace alone, through faith in Jesus and what He accomplished on the cross. (Ephesians 2:8-10).

There's nothing that you can do. Literally nothing.

Grace is free, but it cost Jesus everything. It cost Him His own life. Jesus endured the cross, scorning its shame (Hebrews 12:2), because He wants to say to you, "My child. Come home. Come home."

Have you received His forgiveness for you?

I want you to think about all the junk in your life and everything that brings you shame. But also think about all of the self-righteous things you did right that made you puffed up. The scripture memory, the service, the Bible studies, or any way you tried to earn brownie points.

Write it down. All of it. Read it several times. Endure the weight of what real conviction feels like, the heavy weight on your heart.

Hear me when I say that the Lord didn't die for just your list. He died for your heart. That, my friend, is freedom.

Have you ever sat and experienced what it feels like for His blood to cover your sin? To come to the place where you finally realize you don't have it together and you admit you're a total mess?

The Lord is saying, "*Yes, you are, and you're much messier than you even realize. There's so much more. But you know what? You're mine. You are MINE. I've ransomed you. I have called you by name, and I have died for you.*"

Thank you, Jesus.

Hear me when I say that the Lord didn't die for just your list. He died for your heart. That, my friend, is freedom.

Engage.

Write down all the junk in your life.

What are some things that you do to atone for your own sin?

Will you lay down all the striving and all of the reasons that make you think you're not good enough?

After reading Ezekiel 36:26, is your heart more like stone or more like flesh right now?

Lord, Your Word says, "Do not be afraid, for I have ransomed you. I have called you by name; you are mine" (Isaiah 43:1b). I confess that sometimes I feel that I am Yours and sometimes I don't. Help me to believe that Your Word is true, regardless of how I feel in the moment. And let my feelings catch up to my belief.

6

Sidelined.

Have you ever sat down and read the book of Leviticus?

My bad. Of course you haven't. Let me rephrase that question.

Have you ever tried to sit down and read even a few verses of Leviticus? It's pretty brutal. It's basically a book full of bizarre rules the Israelites had to follow when they were first deemed as God's chosen people.

I often wonder what it would be like if we had to obey the laws of Leviticus today. We would have to memorize twenty-seven chapters chock full of helpful hints, like what to do when your clothes mildew or how to be cleansed from an infectious skin disease.

FYI: Simply burn your moldy tunic. As far as the skin disease goes, you must make a trip to the priest. Don't forget to run over to Target, because you'll need to bring two live birds, some cedar wood, scarlet yarn, and hyssop with you. The ceremony may take a while, so plan on being late to work. (Leviticus 13, 14).

Can you imagine?

We've discussed the perfect lamb that had to be slaughtered for the penalty of sin so justice could be served. A life for a life. That was known as the Day of Atonement and it was the holiest day of the year.

What I didn't mention before is that there were actually two pure lambs. One was killed and the other one was set free. One shouldered our sin and the other shouldered our shame. One spilled blood to cover our sins and the other was burdened with all our shame and led out to the wilderness, never to be seen again.

It's a perfect picture of our Lord. My penalty for my sin is death. He paid that. He paid that for me. But He went a step further and He removed the shame of it.

We have a tendency to forget that part. Does the following scenario ring a bell to you?

I wholeheartedly receive Jesus' forgiveness for my sin. Therefore I know I'm going to heaven. The penalty has been paid in full. I get it. His death erases my sin. I'm truly grateful. Winning.

There's just one problem. If I look closely I can still see the imprint of my list of sins. I still feel the shame of what I did. I'm still walking with a limp, because while I understand that I'm a believer, I am convinced that God still looks at me with disappointment in His eyes. I should have known better. I should have made better choices. So I walk in shame.

Self
Hatred
At
My
Expense

Am I the only one who feels that way?

It cost Jesus everything to set us free. If you walk in shame, you're communicating that the cross wasn't enough.

We must not fall into this trap. It cost Jesus everything to set us free. If you walk in shame, you're communicating that the cross wasn't enough.

Shame keeps me in the shadows and the valleys. It keeps me sidelined when I have a race to run. It's a weight. It's a weight that constantly reminds me that I'm not enough. I'm too much. I'm forgotten. I'm too far gone.

Lies.

Jesus says you are enough. He has called you by name. You are His.

If I allow myself to feel the weight of my sin, then I can fully experience the freedom that comes with forgiveness. I am a frail human who makes a ton of mistakes all day long. You and I need a Savior, not only to get us to heaven, but also to enable us to walk this world in freedom.

The freedom that others see in me is Jesus. It is not Laura. All I have to do is believe Him. The enemy wants me to stay weighted down. But I get to say, "It is finished."

TETELESTAI.

Those were Jesus' last words. "It is finished" (John 19:30). There's no more sacrifice. There's no more debt. There's just one thing left to do.

Believe.

When I was in college, I was a ministry leader at my church. I was a frantic little girl jumping around for God's approval. I was desperate to make myself worthy in His eyes. I lived with Christian roommates. We never drank on the weekends and we weren't sleeping around. We were good girls who spent our Friday nights with high school students, teaching them about Jesus.

I was wasting away, but like Joseph, I had a moment that marked me.

It all began one night as I sat on the curb of Main Street in Navasota, Texas. I was engaged in a conversation with a high school girl who had been drinking since sundown. Needless to say, it was a one way conversation.

She was lamenting over some struggles in her life, many that made her feel unworthy of love. I countered her self-loathing with statements like, "Jesus loves you and wants you to know it. He forgives you and desires an intimate relationship with you. His love is the greatest thing on earth, and you're worthy of it."

Without warning, I had an epiphany. I realized in that moment that while I believed my words to be true, I did not feel them. I was speaking words from my head that in no way had reached my heart and taken hold of my soul.

That next Sunday in church, my pastor said, "Some of you in this room are mad at God. The Lord can handle your anger."

I sat in my pew, shocked. He was talking to me. All I did was tell people how good God is and how much He loves them, yet I was angry. What's even crazier is that I couldn't identify why I was so mad. On top of that, I felt full of shame. You're not supposed to be mad at God. How dare you! Don't tell anyone because they will think you are a horrible person.

In a conversation the next day with my Young Life leader in an office on the Texas A&M campus, seated in another pleather chair, I confessed my predicament. Somewhere along the way, I bit onto the lie that I had to prove my worth to Jesus. I admitted that I was having trouble holding it together, and as I started to unpack my anger, he cut straight to the core when he interrupted me by asking, "Why do you think God saved you?"

He wasn't looking for the right answer. He wanted to know what I really believed.

After a looooong pregnant pause, he filled in some blanks for me. He said, "Do you think it's because you're popular? Maybe it's because you're a twin? Or perhaps because you were a high school cheerleader?"

I was unable to lie and find the "right answer." I was honest and admitted that I thought those were exactly the reasons why He saved me. I had earned my spot on the salvation train and I knew I had to continually prove I was worthy of that spot. I had to work hard to do "Christian" things and stop doing bad things like, well, having fun.

The life I had been leading as a Christian was no more exciting than a root canal and my relationship with Jesus was anything but close and intimate. I didn't really know Him.

He began to lead me through some scriptures that I'd been taught years ago, but somehow never grasped.

He opened his Bible and read Jeremiah 17:9a to me: "The human heart is the most deceitful of all things, and desperately wicked."

He told me I am the woman caught in adultery. I am Zacchaeus who betrayed his friends. I am the woman at the well who has been married five times. I am David who had the affair. I am Moses who didn't believe. I am everyone I see. Why? Because our hearts are all sinful. Sin is sin. Then he asked again, "Why do you think God saved you?"

I didn't know the answer, so he told me.

"Because of the blood of Jesus. The cross is for you. You're telling everybody about it, and you've never stopped to believe it for yourself."

I had never identified as a woman with a sinful heart. I knew I was a woman who had done bad things, but I just needed to try harder, perform better, and Jesus would love me.

As Dr. Phil so famously put it, "How's that working for you?"

I'm a sinner.
I'm forgiven.
I'm free.
I get it.

Y'all, in that moment everything changed for me. Sure, I'd asked Jesus into my heart as a little girl at church camp, but I'm not sure I personally understood my need for a savior. That day, sitting in the pleather chair, the truth finally permeated my heart. The blood that was shed for me, the covering of my sin, my anger, my selfishness, my posing, my inability to connect, my need for everyone and their third cousin's approval, all of it. I just received it.

I'm a sinner. I'm forgiven. I'm free. I get it.

Engage.

Think about a time when you felt ashamed. What kept you in the shadows?

Have you ever allowed Jesus to be your substitutionary atonement?

Do you have the courage to admit that you have been or are currently angry with God? Do you think He can handle it?

Read Romans 3:22. Do you believe? Why do you think God saved you? Be specific.

Jesus, I need You. I've tried everything to remove this wall of sin that separates me from You, and I realize that You're the only one that can remove it. Forgive me, wash me clean, and make me Yours. Come into my life. I'm Yours. Thank You, Father.

7

Indebted.

Once I truly received the forgiveness of Jesus in my own life, I felt the Lord urging me to forgive others. That's when the wheels began to fall off again.

I'm not exaggerating. Forgive all the jokers who have wronged me? Where do I even begin?

Studies have shown that unforgiveness is toxic.[3] It can cause a variety of physical ailments in our lives, as well as emotional distress. Unforgiveness is one of the biggest things that weighs us down. It's one of the primary reasons we are entangled.

Oh, and get this, the Lord doesn't suggest that we forgive. It is not a strong proposition or an important recommendation we should work into our schedule between painting our nails and swinging by the Nordstrom sale over the weekend.

Jesus commands that we forgive. (Ephesians 4:32). It is for our benefit and His glory.

The relationship that the Lord is offering is not a co-pilot situation. (Leviticus 26:12, Jeremiah 30:22). We don't get to share the cockpit with Jesus. We don't call the shots fifty-percent of the time in some feeble halfsies business deal. Jesus says:

I'm your God.
You're My child.
I'm your Father.
You're my kid.
I forgave you.
You forgive others.

Along my pathway in life, when I experience pain, suffering, rejections, betrayals, or someone cutting me off in traffic, that person becomes indebted to me. Does that make sense? When someone hurts me, they owe me. It could be an apology, a way to make it right, a courtesy wave, whatever.

They owe me something.

They're indebted to me.

Case in point. When I was newly pregnant with my son Ben, Jason and I were driving to Houston for a Valentine's Day weekend and we stopped to eat at the Black-Eyed Pea.

No judgement, please. I stand beside The Pea. The pregnant woman wants what the pregnant woman wants.

We enjoyed our savory baby back ribs and hot buttered cornbread and with full bellies, we waddled (okay, I waddled) back to our 1997 Toyota Camry thoroughly satisfied. I noticed the glove compartment was open and there was stuff all over the ground. Everything else seemed intact, but Jason instinctively hopped out of the driver's seat, opened the trunk, and discovered that all of our belongings were gone.

I felt helpless. Standing in the parking lot of the Black-Eyed Pea, I wracked my brain trying to think of ways to make this right as my husband valiantly chose to run down the street in a heroic effort to chase down absolutely no one.

I called the police and the officer on the phone all but laughed at me. He said the area we were in was the highest rate of car burglaries in all of Houston. They would not be sending anyone out, but we could come in person and file a claim.

He may have whispered "sucker" before he hung up the phone.

Jason and I were furious. Justice needed to be served. We had been wronged. They owed us our stuff back. Jason needed his computer. I needed to take their faces and smash them into the pavement so they could hurt like me.

Regrettably, when I incur a loss of some capacity, most of the time there's absolutely nothing I can do about it. I can't do anything to make it right. I can't make them apologize to me. I'm out of control and I don't like that feeling.

Here's what I can do. I can make a list of everyone who has wronged me or anyone who owes me something. BOOM!

It's a long list and I channel my inner Gollum, call it "my precious," and fuss over it for years and years. I fantasize what I would do if I had just five minutes with the jackwagon on the third line of that list. I think about what I would say differently, any actions I may take, enthusiastic hand gestures to really get my point across, you name it.

In reality, I'm projecting what I think justice should look like in each hurtful circumstance. I want that person on his or her knees. I want them looking me in the eye, begging for my forgiveness. I want to make them feel physical or emotional pain so I can observe them hurting like they hurt me.

Have you ever gone Mama Bear on another parent who said something terrible to your child? Have you ever had an argument with a spouse and later replayed the fight in your head to figure out how you could "win" next time? Have you ever wished for the driver flying down the highway, who nearly clipped your side mirror, to get a speeding ticket?

That's your list. *Somehow* the enemy has hooked us to imagine that this list is *somehow* going to bring about justice or *somehow* going to make us stay in control.

What does forgiveness mean again? It means to cancel the debt. When Jesus atoned for my sin as the substitute, He took the debt for me. I owed my life and Jesus paid it for me. When somebody wrongs me or wounds me, Jesus is not denying that that person is indebted. He's not saying that it's no big deal. He's not refuting that there is a debt.

He's asking me to be courageous enough to cancel the debt. That's what forgiveness means.

Jesus is so adamant about me canceling the debt because He knows my list is toxic. It is cancerous and will eventually kill me. It will rob me of freedom. It will suck the life out of me and Jesus is telling me to get rid of it.

"Get rid of all bitterness, rage, anger, harsh words, and slander, as well as all types of evil behavior" (Ephesians 4:31).

Why am I stuck in a bottomless pit?
Why am I so sensitive?
Why is there an edge to my personality all the time?
Why do I secretly delight when others suffer?
Why can't I experience intimacy with my husband?
Why is there so much tension in all of my relationships?
Why can't I just relax?

My little (read: long) list is safe in my own mind. It doesn't impact anybody. It is just between me and me so it doesn't hurt anyone if I obsess about it. All the while, I am running with a limp. I'm hindered in every way. I have grown to believe that the weight is normal and I'm sitting in the church every Sunday, wounded. My friend and I, we gripe about our list, but we also sing the worship songs and occasionally raise our hands.

Jesus wants you to get rid of your list.

I know what you're thinking. You're shaking your head at me right now because your wounds are really, really deep. You've been abused and betrayed by those you trusted the most. Your list is so much more than someone cutting in line or stealing your backpack out of the trunk of your car.

Hear me when I say that your wounds matter to God. THEY MATTER. I am not minimizing your pain. God sees you. He hurts for you.

And let me be clear, forgiveness does not make the sin alright. Sin is sin. What that person did to you was wrong. Just because you forgive doesn't mean that the pain no longer matters. The imprints are still there. Forgiveness is not excusing the other person's behavior.

Forgiveness doesn't make IT okay. Forgiveness makes YOU okay.

Forgiveness is not excusing the other person's behavior. Forgiveness doesn't make IT okay. Forgiveness makes YOU okay.

As you walk through forgiveness, you learn to walk in grace. As I mentioned before, my first year of marriage was anything but happily ever after. The Lord knew that this was the season in my life when He was going to allow all sorts of things to come to the surface.

Intimacy was a struggle. We fought over everything. I was guarded. I was afraid. In any other relationship, I would have run. But I was married and the back door was shut. I wasn't going anywhere and had to face it all head on. The Lord popped me like a zit and I watched as my list squirted out.

Although that's a horrible analogy, it paints an accurate picture of what I was going through.

I thought Jason was my list. I thought he was the source of all my problems. Unbeknownst to me, the Lord used my marriage to squeeze me and force me to really look at my list. Before I could thrive in the healthy marriage I had longed for and prayed for, He had to show me my sickness. I had been walking in unforgiveness for thirty years and never knew it.

So, I decided to forgive Jason and automatically assumed he needed to know that he was forgiven. But wait, should I forgive him if he doesn't own up to his transgressions? What if he disagrees? What if he thinks I'm the one who needs to apologize?

Forgiveness is between me and the Lord. It sets me free because it's a holy act of obedience.

Forgiveness is not an act between me and the person that needs forgiveness. That seems backwards, doesn't it? It's not.

Forgiveness is between me and the Lord. It sets me free because it's a holy act of obedience. That person on my list may never say she is sorry.

But I can still forgive them. I can still walk in obedience.

Nine times out of ten, they're not going to say they're sorry. Eight times out of ten they don't even know they've offended you. They're not even thinking about you.

Renowned Christian author and theologian Lewis Smedes, an expert on the topic of forgiveness, says, "When we forgive evil we do not excuse it, we do not tolerate it, we do not smother it. We look the evil full in the face, call it what it is, let its horror shock and stun and enrage us, and only then do we forgive it."[4]

Well said.

Engage.

Do you ever feel that Jesus is your co-pilot?

Read Ephesians 4:31 once more. Write down the ways you struggle with bitterness, rage, anger, harsh words, and slander.

Have you ever considered that sin is between you and the Lord? How have your viewpoints changed since reading this study?

Christian author Max Lucado said, "Forgiveness is unlocking the door to set someone free and realizing that you were the prisoner."[5] What is your reaction to this quote?

Lord, I desire to be so connected with You that Your prayer "Forgive us our debts, as we forgive our debtors" (Matthew 6:12 NKJV), is a reality in my own life. I pray that this charge becomes my battle cry. With a grateful spirit I bow my heart before You, trusting You to enable me to freely love, freely forgive.

8

List.

Okay, who wants to dig your mental list out of the crevices of your brain and write it down on an old-fashioned piece of paper!

Don't be afraid. This is exciting stuff. Why?

Because it's freedom.

Start with categories.

The first type of hurt is intentional. It's a direct hurt. Begin with the people who deliberately hurt you. The ones who plotted the pain, like Joseph's brothers who sold him into slavery.

Think about the one who left you. The one who abused you. The one who rejected you. It's a purposeful, direct hit coming straight towards you.

People are messy. We're broken. We're sinful and we hurt people.

People are messy. We're broken. We're sinful and we hurt people. Many of us have suffered at the hand of abusers, whether it be physical abuse, sexual abuse, verbal abuse, emotional abuse. Parents have abandoned you. Friends have betrayed you. It was an intended hurt, and we must look it full in the face with courage because it matters to God.

The second type of hurt is unintentional. It's an indirect hurt. Take Joseph again. He is rejected, falsely accused by Potiphar's wife, and thrown into prison. That's a direct hurt. But, there's a cupbearer in prison with Joseph who has a dream. Joseph has been given favor by God to interpret the dream and when the cupbearer is reinstated to his position of power, Joseph asks him to vouch for him to Pharaoh. He says, "Remember me!" (Genesis 40).

Scripture says the cupbearer gets out of prison, and "forgot all about Joseph, never giving him another thought" (Genesis 40:23). He forgot all about him and Joseph sat in prison for another two years. That is an indirect hit. The cupbearer didn't get out and plot anything against Joseph. He's just self-absorbed, living his life.

I live with a human. There are times in my mind I want Jason to come in and notice that I got my hair cut a month ago. He still to this day hasn't noticed. I can brood over my list thinking that Jason doesn't care about me or see me. It's an indirect hurt if I let it fester.

My parents got divorced when I was thirteen. I remember the day my mother told me. I was sitting at the kitchen bar eating an English muffin for breakfast. She turned off the television and with tears in her eyes shared the news that would change all of our lives forever. Now, did my mom wake up that morning and think to herself, "I wonder how I can take Laura out today? I know, I'll get divorced." No. Obviously that wasn't her train of thought or the motive of her heart. My mom loves me with every fiber of her being. I know that. But I didn't come out of that divorce unscathed. None of us did. Her decision affected me personally. That's an indirect hurt.

Growing up, my dad could have had conversations with me to make sure I didn't need the approval of boys. But he didn't. Did he love me? You better believe he did. Oh, my goodness, did he love me. Does that make it okay? No. He should have protected me. He should have set me up for success in a way that only a father can with his daughter. Again, indirect hurt.

I carried the weight of it all. So my dad is on my list. My mom is on my list. And Jason is on my list.

It was twenty years ago when I asked the Lord to show me who is on my list. He brought to mind a childhood acquaintance that had been on my list for years. We never had a falling out, I don't even remember a cross word between us, but she hurt a friend of mine.

I'm sure their rift was over something super serious like which brand of jeans were better, Lovetts or Jordache. That's not my point. My point is, when you hurt my friend, you hurt me.

She had been on my list for years and I didn't know it. If you had asked me if I liked this girl, I would have said yes, of course. But, I remember coming home from college and when our high school girlfriends got together, I found it difficult to be around her, and I'm not sure I could have told you why at the time.

When it was revealed that she was on my list, I blew it off. That was twenty-five years ago and we don't even live in the same town anymore.

Those are just details. It doesn't matter if you have daily contact with the person on your list. If a name is on it, the weight is there and it will hinder your race. Get rid of it.

There are also names on your list that you are hesitant to write down because it feels like a betrayal. Newsflash: Your parents, your siblings, and your kids will be on this list. My kids are twelve and ten-years-old. My son made my list when he was a toddler.

This is a safe list. Don't waste one minute feeling some false sense of guilt.

There will even be people on your list who have died. It seems crazy, but it's true. A relative who abused you. The loss of a parent that felt like abandonment to you. A friend who passed away and you never received closure in the relationship.

This is a safe list. Don't waste one minute feeling some false sense of guilt. That's exactly where the enemy wants you. If you are too scared or too proud or too ashamed to truly be honest with the names on your list, he wins. You'll still be running with a limp. You'll be weighed down. You will be entangled.

But if you run full force the way the Lord intended you to run, you're a threat to the enemy. When we run in freedom, we push back the darkness. If you hear whispers telling you that you are selfish for writing a certain name down, write it down. Don't analyze it.

Let me ask you a question. Are you going to put your own name on the list? Do you feel the weight of your own depravity?

Here's the deal. Until you've been flattened by the overwhelming grace of God in your own life, you can't freely give it out. You put yourself on the list because you need to be there. You also take yourself off the list. Why? Because the cross paid for it. That's grace.

> The gospel is this: We are more sinful and flawed in ourselves than we ever dared believe, yet at the very same time we are more loved and accepted in Jesus Christ than we ever dared hope.[6]
> —Timothy J. Keller

As soon as I think I'm killing it as an upstanding Christian woman, I scream at my kids on the way to school. As soon as I plan to turn the TV off and read my Bible, a new season of *Call the Midwife* gets released. Forget my responsibilities, I've got an appointment with Netflix. As soon as I've returned my last impulsive purchase, Gap offers forty-percent off for Friends & Family. I continually miss the mark and I'm on my list.

I'm a mess. So are you. But, I'm overcome by the goodness of God when I look my own junk right in the face. None of us have it all together. You don't and nobody thinks you do. If we all just began to confess why we're on our list, we'd be wrecked. But none of us would be surprised.

None of us.

You know who else is on your list? God.

That's right. I said it. God is on your list.

But read these next sentences very carefully. God does not need your forgiveness. God has never wronged you. He is holy, He is loving, He is just, and He is merciful.

My expectations of God have often led me to disappointment. He has not jumped through the hoops that I wanted Him to jump through. He has not healed when I have asked Him to. He has not moved in the way I have wanted Him to move. There are things I have begged God to do and He hasn't done them, which made me disappointed and then angry. Because of that anger, He is on my list, and you better believe that's going to trip me up.

Hey, you. The Lord can handle your anger.

Some of us have never had the permission just to be honest with the Lord. If you read through the Psalms, you'll see David crying out to the Lord all the time. Why? When? How? How long?

There is something spiritual that takes place when I come into the holy place of just me and the Lord and I say, "This is the real truth." It gives God room to work and He begins to move. Most times, I don't get the answers that I initially come seeking.

But I get Him. I get His presence.

Part of what the cross paid for and afforded me is that I get to come into my Father's house at any time and say, "Dad, why? Why? Stop. Make it stop. Change it. Fix it now."

The Lord says, *"Laura, you just come. All of you who you are weary and heavy burdened, you just come. Take a deep breath. I'm still going to move the way I meant to move. There are things that you don't understand, that you're never going to understand, but when you get Me and you taste and you see that I'm good, you're going to take a deep breath and you're going to be okay."*

Engage.

Find a quiet place where you won't be interrupted. Take a deep breath and spend the next thirty minutes creating your list. Ask the Lord, "Who is on my list?" Don't analyze the names or become frustrated when it doesn't make sense. Simply write it out.

Jesus, would You reveal to me the ways I'm weighing myself down? Help me to push back the darkness. Help me to run in freedom. You are my refuge in whom I trust. I am weary. I am burdened. And I am ready to have a conversation. Just You and me.

9

Steps.

Now that you have your list (eighteen pages front and back), it's time to do something with it. Are you ready to feel a weight lifted? Are you ready to run?

In some instances, it's simple to remove people from your list. You forgive, draw a line through their name, and it's done. It's over. Victory.

Others will take a little more effort. Or perhaps you finally remove them from your list and they eventually bounce back with new offenses. I'm looking at you, husbands, parents, kids, and close friends.

Forgiving isn't easy, but there are five steps that can be taken to help us trust God through the process:

Tell.
Feel.
Cancel.
Accept.
Risk.

These steps are not magical. They are not the be-all, end-all. They are a tool that the Holy Spirit uses to encourage us to surrender.

I want to reiterate that in no way, shape, or form do I minimize the hurt and the wounds that you have suffered. Some wounds are unthinkable. Unimaginable. It's not about erasing a name off your list and suddenly your life is neat and tidy. It's not about forgiving and forgetting the pain.

It's not.

Forgiveness is an act of obedience and an act of faith between you and the Lord. You're making a decision to cancel the debt. It's not an emotion.

Forgiveness is an act of obedience and an act of faith between you and the Lord. You're making a decision to cancel the debt. It's not an emotion. Known for her heart of reconciliation, Jesus warrior and author Corrie ten Boom said, "Forgiveness is an act of the will, and the will can function regardless of the temperature of the heart."[7]

If I step out in obedience and in faith, regardless of how I feel, the Lord honors that decision.

Do you know the best part? When my emotions finally do catch up (and be aware, it can take time, sometimes a lot of time), it solidifies the healing. It affirms the process. Another victory.

Take a moment to think about your list. Choose one person. Do you have the name? Can you see a face? I want you to keep that person in mind as we begin to unpack our tools. You ready? Here we go.

Engage.

Unbelief pervades our thinking, so we often have to meditate on the things that are true about God. (Philippians 4:8). Confront unbelief by rehearsing what is true about the Lord: You are sovereign and in control. You are good and You love me. You are with me (or, rather, I am with You). You are working in me "to will and to act in order to fulfill *Your* good purpose" (Philippians 2:13 NIV).

> The heart is hard and the memory slippery, and without meditation all is lost; meditation imprints and fastens a truth in the mind. Without meditation the truths which we know will never affect our hearts.[8]
> —Thomas Watson

Before you move on to the next chapter and begin with step one, sit before the Lord and take a deep breath. Visualize yourself taking His hand and allowing Him to walk you through each one of the steps of forgiveness.

Jesus, I'm taking a moment to pause, to be still and know that You are God. (Psalm 46:10). You are the Great Healer. You are Jehovah Rapha. I can trust You with this process. Lead me as I obey You.

10

Tell.

Share each hurt with God. Name them all.

"Give all your worries and cares to God, for He cares about you" (1 Peter 5:7).

Excellent. Where do I begin? Let me go get my Burn Book and we'll start right away.

I know that's an excellent use of pop culture vernacular from the movie *Mean Girls*, but the Lord really does care about the things or people who have injured you. Acknowledge the hurts to God. Not just the big ones or the tragic ones.

All of them.

Why do you have to recount every one? Because it builds your relationship with God.

But doesn't He already know everything, including your hurts? Yes, He does.

I like to sit before the Lord and old school text. It's very powerful when I see the words staring back at me.

I like to sit before the Lord and old school text. That means I take pen to paper and write everything out. It's very powerful when I see the words staring back at me. I found it to be more helpful than mentally ticking off injustices.

Give all your worries and cares to Him. Remember, He cares for you. Be brutally honest.

What's the hurt?
Write it down.
She left me.
He abused me.
It was slander.
Be specific.
Does this violation suddenly feel petty?
Sin is sin.
Write it down.
A wound is a wound.
Name it.
Say it out loud.
Write it down.

Engage.

Find a quiet place where you won't be interrupted. Look at your list and acknowledge your hurts to God. You don't have to blow through your list all at once.

Take your time.

Go slow.

Choose one person.

Write down the reason they are on your list. If you have several reasons, write them all down. Then move on to the next one.

Lord, bring to mind every hurt, every offense, every wound. I'm a little scared to go there with You, but I'm trusting that freedom is worth it. Your perfect love will drive out my fear and Your steadfast presence will be my courage. So have Your way, bring to mind all that I need to remember and tell You.

11

Feel.

Tell God how the hurt made you feel. Grieve it.

This part makes us afraid. This is why we sit in that hospital waiting room with a hemorrhaging leg and our friends just engage with us, because it's so awkward and scary to go to that place of pain. We're afraid we'll never come out of it.

I dread this step. I think if I really open myself up and relive those dark days, I'll stay there forever. Or I'll drown underneath it. I won't be able to recover. It's better for me to tiptoe around on the surface of the hurt. I don't care if there's an elephant in the room. I can voice my pain, but don't make me feel it. I barely made it through the first time they hurt me. Why would I want to go through that again?

Who's been there with me?

Let me give you an example of a time I was indirectly hurt by someone I deeply trusted and admired. It was the summer of 1989 and I was planning to work at a camp in Colorado. I needed three references in order for my application to be accepted. One of those references came from a trusted spiritual leader and mentor of mine.

I honestly don't remember how I got my hands on his feedback, but I did.

It wasn't rosy like I thought it would be. I just remember reading the phrase, "Laura can be overbearing at times."

I'm sorry, what?

At forty-seven that's not a hard pill to swallow, but at seventeen, it was crushing. His approval meant more to me than it probably should have and reading that review became more than feedback. It was an indictment. I might as well have the word OVERBEARING stamped on my forehead for all the world to see. Sure, I was an impressionable teenager with daddy issues, but his words hurt. Deeply. At seventeen I adopted a new identity. Overbearing.

It seems petty, right? I didn't even plan to write it down, but I trusted the Holy Spirit through this process, and when I began to write out and acknowledge my hurt to God, I sensed Him gently prompting me. *"How did it make you feel?"*

I went back to seventeen year-old Laura, and I wept. I wept for lots of reasons. I felt misunderstood. Labeled. Rejected. There's the wound.

That word, overbearing, stayed in my mind for years whenever I thought of myself. I allowed one opinion to mark me for far too long. It made me timid to speak up when God had given me a voice to use for His glory. I avoided ministry positions for years because I assumed I was too, (you guessed it) overbearing.

I grieved before the Lord.
All the worries.
All the cares.
All the pain.

Then I sat there with the Lord, and I grieved my relationship with this mentor, and I grieved the relationship I never had with my dad. I allowed myself to cry and remember every bit of that pain of feeling lost and in need of an engaged father. I grieved before the Lord. All the worries. All the cares. All the pain.

You must grieve it. Don't downplay it. Don't minimize it to self protect. Go there. Go there with the knowledge that you will not stay there. You won't, but it's a necessary place to get to healing.

In Psalm 23:4 (ESV) David says, "Even though I walk through the valley of the shadow of death, I will fear no evil, for you are with me."

At first glance, it may appear that David is on death's doorstep. That's not the case in this passage. When he was young, David was a shepherd and when winter came, he would take his sheep to a higher pasture where the grass hadn't been eaten by the flocks. In order to get to there, David had to go down into a dangerous valley where robbers could hide out and his sheep could be hunted by predators. It was a difficult and scary journey.

David didn't camp out in the valley, but he did have to go through it to get to the other side. If he stayed down there, he would die. So he pressed on.

It's the same with us. You must go through the pain to get to the other side. So many of us don't know that we'll survive that valley, so we refuse to go there. We're scared. We stay in that hospital waiting room with a hemorrhaging leg having happy hour with our friends wondering why we're not acting normal, wondering why our anxiety is off the charts.

I understand that it's scary. It was for me too. But I can tell you firsthand that a new day is coming. You'll get up and through it.

The grass on the other side is much greener. It's worth it.

Engage.

Now give yourself some time to feel the pain of each transgression. Cry out to the Lord. Remember how it hurt. Stop holding on to your hemorrhaging leg. Talk about the elephant in the room. Grieve as long as you need to grieve.

Give all your worries to God. He cares for you.

He does.

Something to think about. None of us are meant to journey through life alone. As imperfect as people are, we all need a few trusted friends around us with whom we can share our journey. Sometimes among those friends we may need a pastor or professional counselor who can help us navigate the most difficult parts of the journey. The wisest and healthiest people take advantage of wise counsel and the prayerful encouragement of friends.

Lord, Your Word promises me that I am not alone in this pain. You invite me to come boldly to Your throne of grace and You meet me with such mercy, such grace to hold me in my hurt. (Hebrews 4:16). I trust that You are with me, that You love me. Comfort me in ways only You can.

12

Cancel.

Cancel the debt.
Mark the debtor off your list.

We're heading into tricky waters, so be on guard. The next step can be emotional, but it can't be based in emotions. It's an act of obedience. This is the part of our journey when the enemy whispers the lie that forgiveness means you are allowing the person on your list to "get away" with their behavior or you are somehow condoning their actions.

Don't fall into that temptation.

Initially, you'll start scratching easy ones off your list. Former bosses, old grudges, and petty grievances. You'll move on to the "biggies." But don't be surprised when they bounce back onto your list.

What about you? To keep yourself on the list is saying to Jesus, "Your cross is enough for her, but not enough for me." You must forgive yourself. You must forgive yourself if you are on your list.

Here's what IS NOT happening. While acknowledging the debt to God and admitting your feelings related to that debt, you say the magic words and POOF! It disappears into oblivion before you move to the following debtor. Next!

No. This is what's really happening.

While acknowledging the debt to God and admitting your feelings related to that debt, you take it to the cross and lay it on Christ's shoulders. He gets to deal with it. The imprints are still there, but it's no longer yours to carry.

Thank you, Jesus.

Think of it this way: You're shopping at Walmart and you place travel shampoo bottles, a bag of chips, and the latest *People Magazine* in your buggy. After tossing a dozen other things you don't need in the basket, you roll up to the counter to check out. Don't forget a package of Trident cinnamon gum.

Question: Who owns the stuff in your basket?

Walmart owns it. You haven't paid for it yet. But when you do swipe your debit card, the items become yours. They don't hold onto the items, you take it all away.

Jesus paid for our sins and our iniquities. He owns them. If I'm gripping it so tightly because justice needs to be served, I'm stealing what He already paid for. It's His debt.

And I'm going to let Him take it.

I no longer have the strength to carry it. I'm not savvy enough to figure out how to fix it. I can't heal myself. I'm not going to demand payment. I have no idea how justice will be served. But I will trust Jesus since it cost Him everything for me to relinquish this burden.

I've made the decision to cancel the debt.

Yes! Good for you!

Now, what will you do when you give it all to God and He doesn't do anything with it right away? Are you going to sit back and stare at Him until He makes it right? Did you do something wrong in step three? Should you go pick the debt back up again?

Leave it there. This step is all about surrendering your right to own what is not yours. You've given it to the Lord, who already paid for it. It's His. Take the name off the list.

This step is all about surrendering your right to own what is not yours. You've given it to the Lord, who already paid for it.

She's Yours, Lord. He's Yours, too. I'm canceling the debt.

Kudos my friend! You've done it! You're going to let God deal with it. Hooray! What do you think the punishment will be?

Wait, what? Are we allowed to ask that?

Admit it. Your mind went there. It's a natural place to go since scripture says there will always be consequences for our sins. But the Lord defines what justice looks like when you cancel the debt. We trust God with our list and He will work out the details.

When we get to heaven, it will all makes sense.

Engage.

As you ponder the Walmart analogy, ask yourself this: What's in my basket that He's already paid for?

Are there people and hurts that I need to give back to their rightful owner, Jesus?

What is it that keeps you from fully surrendering certain debts?

Have you cancelled the debt against yourself?

Lord, guide me to hear the Spirit of truth over the mumbling lies that hold me back from surrendering what I no longer need to carry. Show me what I'm trying to hold onto that You've already paid for on the cross. Through the mighty power of Your great love and compassion, give me the courage to release it back to You.

13

Accept.

See the person as they are. They may never change.

Here's the beauty of forgiveness: When we forgive, it changes our perspective. Like I said before, forgiveness doesn't make the hurt okay. It makes me okay. When I can choose to accept the person on my list, just as they are, I can move forward.

Philippians 4:19 has helped me move forward. "And this same God who takes care of me will supply all your needs from His glorious riches, which have been given to us in Christ Jesus."

This means that God sees the gaps in my life caused by broken relationships. These are the emotional needs that don't get met by mom or dad. He brings along a pastor, coach, or friend to provide support at just the right moment. Believers in Christ are like family. I've got countless spiritual moms, dads, sisters, and brothers. Each one provides something only God knows I need. He sees you.

So what about the abusive people who have to be in your life for extenuating circumstances? The ones who aren't going anywhere? What about the addicts? What about the unhealthy relationships?

We all have to learn to set boundaries. I have to ask the Lord, "What does this look like for me? Do we stay together? Do we separate?"

There are relationships that are no longer in my life because they are unhealthy. I'm not harboring bitterness toward them. I can pray for them, I can even wish them well, but I will never be controlled by them again.

My advice is to concentrate on the freedom that comes when you no longer carry them around. You've given them to the Lord. You've forgiven them. Don't expect anything from them. Don't demand they stand up and come to the plate like they should have a long time ago.

Take it to the cross.

When I forgave my mom, it was like I could see clearly for the first time. I saw the single woman who worked so hard to provide for my siblings and me. There was gratitude, grace, and peace.

Smedes said, "You will know that forgiveness has begun when you recall those who hurt you and you feel the power to wish them well."[9] That power comes from the Holy Spirit through the obedient act of forgiveness.

Power comes from the Holy Spirit through the obedient act of forgiveness.

I want you to feel that power.

Engage.

How does it feel to know that you and I don't have the power to really change another person?

Will you trust God to work on the people in your life that need to change, or grow or get healed? What would that look like?

Will you trust God to work in your own life to bring about real change and transformation? What would that look like?

As you walk in obedience, learning to accept those that you forgave, how is your perspective changing?

Jesus, I am humbled by Your passion to mend my brokenness and my broken relationships. You stand in the gap and supply my every need. Oh Jesus, You are enough. I can trust You with those I hold most dear and with those that most need changing. Even if they never change, You are enough for me.

14

Risk.

Risk being hurt again. Run your race.

Jason and I were on staff at a church several years ago and we experienced a very painful departure from it. Guess what? Church people are messy, too. It felt like we got punched in the gut, totally thrown off balance.

After some time, I walked through forgiveness and laid it down completely. What I didn't realize though, is that I had built a self-protective wall in my heart against the church, any church. I avoided leadership positions for five years. Then the Lord worked in my heart and I began to seek community again, recognizing that while messy and sometimes dysfunctional, the church is the bride of Christ, and I'm part of it.

When Jason was offered a position on staff at a new church, my breath caught. What if I get hurt again? It was too painful. I can't go down that road another time.

This step is important because you are showing the Lord that you completely trust Him. You're not going to sit on the

This step is important because you are showing the Lord that you completely trust Him.

sidelines because you are scared. You're going to risk being hurt again because you have walked through forgiveness and you are free.

Does that mean you dive right into another abusive relationship because you forgave the first one? No. You have to set healthy boundaries. For some of us, we need extra help in understanding how to play that out. May I suggest Christian counseling?

Asking for help is a sign of strength that you recognize your hemorrhaging leg. You acknowledge the weight that hinders you from running your race. It's proof that you trust the Lord to shine a light on the darkness.

Have you always been told that counseling is a sign of weakness?

Rebuke that thought. Tell Satan to get behind you.

Now what?

You're gonna love this. We get to wait on the Lord. Isn't that fun? We are so lucky to be living in a generation that is super patient.

Please read that last sentence with a sarcastic tone.

There are dozens and dozens of verses about waiting on the Lord. Hosea tells us to wait how long? Always. (Hosea 12:6 NIV). Way to be detail-oriented, Hosea. Our shepherd friend David wants us to not only wait patiently, but we have to be still while doing it. (Psalm 37:7). Right. Paul wants us to wait eagerly, which shouldn't be a problem in this day and age. (1 Corinthians 1:7).

My point is that God is going to have His way in His time. And we have to be cool with that.

We serve a God that is a God of reconciliation. Nine times out of ten, when I've walked through the steps of forgiveness, reconciliation has come. I've not orchestrated it. I've not manipulated it. I've just waited.

If He wants to reconcile the relationship, He will.

You may desperately long to be reconciled or you fall on the side of being terrified to death that you may have to reconcile. Either way, walk through the steps of forgiveness and trust Jesus to bring it about in His time.

Remember, He cares for you.

Isaiah 40:11 reminds us that, "He will carry the lambs in His arms, holding them close to His heart." That's what I've experienced to be true as I've made strides in this level of obedience through forgiveness.

Our Father is tender. Especially when we're dealing with the consequences of our own sins.

There's a story about King David and Bathsheba in the Old Testament. He had an affair with Bathsheba. Then he had her husband killed. David made a total mess of his life and he lost his son because of it. It was one of the consequences. (2 Samuel 11-12:24).

But after David grieved the death of his son, he got up, he received the consequence, and he moved on. King David is famously known in scripture as a friend of God and a man after God's own heart. (Acts 13:22).

Don't ever count yourself out. Don't ever think that you've made too many mistakes or been on the receiving end of too many wrongs that you can't figure out a way to run. There's always space to run freely again.

Don't ever count yourself out. There's always space to run freely again.

God is a redeeming God. Not only does He want to redeem your heart, but He wants to redeem your past, too. We have to understand that when we receive His forgiveness for our own sin, it empowers us to extend it to others.

After Hurricane Harvey came and sat on Houston for days, my sister Catherine and her kids lived with us for three months. It was crowded and chaotic, but it was also a sweet time. I realized at that moment that we could easily be sister wives.

Instead of calling Jason to talk about dinner, I called Catherine. Instead of calling Jason to talk about carpool, I called Catherine. We just kind of developed a rhythm.

After they moved out, I noticed some tension between Jason and me. In other words, he was dancing on my last nerve. I was easily offended and everything was a struggle. I quickly realized that he was back on my list.

Lord knows I was on his list, too.

I pulled out my trusty legal pad and I wrote down Jason's name, what he did, and how it made me feel. I went through all the steps.

We had small group that night. I hadn't seen him all day. As soon as he walked in, I melted. I saw him differently. Something lifted. I knew then that this was a spiritual, powerful process. I apologized immediately.

Relationships are tough. We're dealing with difficult people, unbelievers, or those who are wrapped up in addiction. I want you to know that you can thrive. You can forgive and you can run unhindered. Pray that God gets ahold of that man or that woman and does a work in his or her life that only He can do.

Trust the Lord to bring the healing. Reconciliation may or may not be possible, but forgiveness doesn't depend on it.

Engage.

Are you aware of self-protective walls that you put up with others and with God? Describe them.

Walking through forgiveness brings us freedom. Do your relational boundaries need work to guard your freedom? Be specific.

If reconciliation is slow to come or never comes, what do you do with your feelings? Do you ever vent to God?

Read Isaiah 30:18. List the ways this verse gives you hope.

Lord, the most exciting place to be is in the midst of Your will. Lead me. As I step out in faith again, remind me that You are my Protector, my Healer, my Guide. Give me discernment, wisdom and courage to follow You with my whole heart. You tenderly bless me as I wait on You.

15

Question.

In order to teach on a topic like forgiveness, I had to clock in a significant amount of personal time on the subject matter. While I have not perfected the art of forgiveness, I have used the last couple of decades looking to the Lord for guidance to help me understand.

Consider me your fun-loving guinea pig.

But before we move on, I'd like to address some common questions that may be rolling around in your brain. No, I'm not an alumni of Hogwarts, although I totally would have been in the Gryffindor house. I've just been doing this for a very long time and the same concerns always seem to pop up time and time again.

Allow me to walk you through a few of them.

Do you recommend we try to knock off the little ones on our list first? Or go for the big daddy?

> I think you should do whatever feels the best to you. If you want to feel a little successful hitting up those who you know won't be so bad, go for it. Some of us prefer to dive right on into the deep end. Others just want to dip a toe in first and then ease our way down the list. Do it however you want. Just do it.

If you were really hurt and you know you should give it to Jesus to reconcile, should you reach out to that person?

What I have learned over the years is that you should wait. Then you wait some more. My personality is to grab the reins because I'm afraid that person may not want to reconcile. I end up making the phone call prematurely when I'm not really ready to have the conversation. I learned this the hard way, so I choose to wait and wait and wait. I let the Lord bring the conversation about. That way I know He's in control and I'm not.

I can rest, knowing that the Lord sees my heart and understands that I want more than anything to be back in fellowship with that person. But I also want it to be right. So I continue to share that burden with Him and trust Him the best I can.

But there are other times when the Lord may be inviting me to make the phone call and I really don't want to. In that instance, I pray through it.

And how exactly do you pray through it?

Well, I start by asking the Lord to strike them down and then take them out. After I calm down a bit, I admit that everything feels wrong and that I'm hurting. I follow up asking questions like David did. "Why did this happen? How could she have done that? Who does she think she is?"

That often morphs into vindication, which comes from an emotionally raw place that hasn't yet been healed. Here's where the shame of, *"I shouldn't feel this way,"* comes into play. So I feel all the feels, but I don't act on anything.

Eventually, I trust Him. I watch as the Lord changes my heart and my perspectives. Then I celebrate what the Lord has done in my life. I can wish this person well and come to a place of healing, knowing it all falls under the cross.

What if I don't want to forgive?

I say this with all respect because I've been in that same place. This is a pride issue and you're being disobedient. However, the beautiful thing is that the Lord is not asking me to get to a place of wanting to forgive.

The Lord is just asking me to forgive.

Never have I walked through the steps of forgiveness feeling like I wanted to. Not one time. In fact, I often go kicking and screaming. The Lord is not dependent and He is not disappointed that I don't feel like it. He just wants me to make me well.

You're never going to feel ready. Look at the cross. That's all you need to see. Let that be enough. That blood has covered you. While you in your flesh don't have the power, the Spirit in you does. The Lord will take it on if You trust Him.

Is obedience better than sacrifice?

Obedience is coming from a place of belief. It doesn't necessarily mean that obedience is coming from a place of excitement or happiness. I can be in a state of grief, of mourning, of woundedness, but my obedience is belief. Believing His Word is true.

It's like the dad in Mark 9:24 who said, "I do believe, but help me overcome my unbelief!" Ditto to that statement, am I right? God knows that we're weak and we're frail. But when I step out in obedience, He blesses me. That's when I have the most joy.

Why is toxic such a buzzword? Aren't we all sinners?

Toxic relationships drain life instead of give life. Toxicity is present when it's choking the life out of you, when there's no freedom, and it's unhealthy. It's hard to even explain it, but you know that it's not okay.

The Spirit has given me a discernment to recognize red flags. I might not know why, I just know there's a flag in my gut. Sometimes, He's used a wise counselor to help me identify them. When this happens, I take caution without needing to understand why. I step back. I trust the Lord. I'm not responsible for them. They're responsible. The Lord is responsible. I can pray for them, but I'm not going to saddle up next to them.

Father, help me to continue to ask the tough questions. Because of Your steadfast love for me, I call out to You and I trust that You will answer, teaching me deep and unsearchable truths. (Jeremiah 33:3). Your understanding and direction guide my acts of obedience. I believe. Please, Lord, will You help my unbelief?

16

Trust.

I want to focus on something we touched on in Chapter 8. What happens if God is on your list?

By the way, if God is not on your list, I'm happy for you. I'd also like to encourage you not to skip this chapter, because if you give it a little more time, He will eventually get there.

Scripture says, "If you love me, obey my commandments" (John 14:15). Repeatedly we read those words in reverse. We think that God is saying, "If you love me now, you're going to obey me." The actual interpretation is to love God means to obey God.

We take Him at His word and jump off the cliff in a free fall. We surrender. We give Him our life. We walk in close fellowship. We mistakenly think we will never be disappointed because we chose to give Him our hearts.

When Beth was born with the congenital heart issue, I wanted God to heal it. In my mind, He would supernaturally touch her heart and the hole would close. She would not need surgery. I walked with Him for three and a half years wanting, begging, asking Him to heal hear. And I believed He would.

He did not.

She had surgery, and thank God, she's doing great. But that was tough for me. I was leaning in with all I had and it felt like God dropped the ball.

As I walk with the Lord, there are going to be times when my heart desires something, and my flesh convinces my brain that I'm not going to be okay if the desire isn't met. When that happens, I set up an expectation on God. I subconsciously figure He must do this for me to be okay and for me to really believe that He is good and cares for me.

God is good. He is sovereign. The two are never mutually exclusive. But He is never going to jump through the hoop of my expectations. Never.

His sovereignty will leave lots of unanswered questions for me. But if I only believe what my eyes see, He does not seem good some of the time. He just doesn't.

Therefore, if I am to fix my eyes on Jesus, I've got to ask Him to open my eyes to show me what I don't see on my own. Show me what I can't understand on my own. Give me a glimpse into what He's doing.

Fair warning: God isn't going to show me every single little detail and how this piece of the puzzle may look tragic now, but it actually fits into this bigger piece that all culminates into a beautiful masterpiece.

Again, these are things I plan on discussing in great detail as I sip my chai tea in the Heavenly Starbucks.

But until we get there with our complimentary punch card, I must walk by faith and not by sight. I identify this tragic piece, I accept that I don't know what the bigger picture is, and I decide to trust

I decide to trust the truth that while this isn't good, He's going to work it into good.

the truth that while this isn't good, He's going to work it into good. (Romans 8:28).

We're going to take a look at how this is lived out in the lives of two women that I have come to love. John 12:1-8 tells the story.

Mary, Martha, and Lazarus are siblings living in the village of Bethany. They are in Jesus' inner circle and He loved them dearly.

We learn that Mary anointed Jesus with very expensive perfume and wiped His feet with her hair. I know this sounds strange, but it truly was an act of worship. It was a huge deal for Mary to dump an entire bottle of Chanel No. 5 on Jesus' toes. That would have been a year's worth of wages.

Judas, the disciple who betrayed Jesus, freaked out and chastised Mary. The expensive perfume was a small fortune. They could have sold it and given the money to the poor. Or the wicked Judas could have pocketed the change. Details.

Jesus defended Mary. He said, "Leave her alone. She did this in preparation for My burial. You will always have the poor among you, but you will not always have Me."

Mary understood something in the spiritual realm that the rest of the group didn't understand in the natural realm. She understood that this wasn't just a gift for Jesus. She didn't bless Him with a warm loaf of banana bread. She cracks open her life savings and she pours it at her Savior's feet because she understands what is about to happen.

There's an intimacy that we are already seeing with Mary and Jesus that takes her to the end of the race. Mary is the one standing at Jesus' tomb. Many assert Mary is the first one Jesus speaks to when He rises from the dead. He looks at her and He calls her by name. (John 20:11-16).

"Mary Magdalene found the disciples and told them, 'I have seen the Lord!' Then she gave them His message" (John 20:18). A woman, preaching the gospel. Go figure. Why? Because she knew what it meant to fix her eyes on Jesus. Let's keep going.

In John 11:2-4 (NIV), we're told that Lazarus was sick, so the sisters sent word to Jesus that, "the one You love is sick." When Jesus heard, He said, "This sickness will not end in death. No, it is for God's glory so that God's Son may be glorified through it."

In the natural realm, there is a crisis. Lazarus is sick and he may not recover and he needs to be healed. Mary and Martha reach out to their BFF and present their need. They want healing and they want it now.

Jesus recognizes the need, but explains there's a bigger story in the spiritual realm. It's going to bring God glory and it's the best thing for everyone involved.

Yeah, Mary and Martha don't really care about the big plan. Can't their friend, the friend Who performs miracles all the time, just heal their brother already?

God can heal. God does heal. But when God doesn't heal, we are faced with disappointment. We can't be guilty of promising something that God will do when we, in our fallibility, don't fully know.

Let's be good stewards when we're sitting on the hospital floor with the hemorrhaging friend of ours. Let's point the friend to Jesus, the One Who understands more than I understand.

Jesus says we should pray and ask for healing. He says lay hands and heal. He says anoint the sick with oil. We're going to do that. And we're going to continue to ask for healing until we see earthly healing or they are healed in heaven.

I love that I get to come to Him with all these questions, and my anger, and my disappointment, and say, "Help me make sense of this."

The Lord is so gracious. I don't have that level of power to manipulate Him. What I do have is the level of power to do what He has asked me to do. I'm a vessel in His hands. He's not a vessel in my hands. Do you see how it gets flipped very quickly? We lose sight of that. So we must be careful that our hearts stay in a posture of surrender at all times. I love that I get to come to Him with all these questions, and my anger, and my disappointment, and say, "Help me make sense of this."

"Now, Jesus loved Martha and her sister and Lazarus. So when He heard that Lazarus was ill, He stayed two days longer in the place where He was" (John 11:5-6 ESV).

H-A-R-S-H.

Jesus is probably on Martha and Mary's speed dial. When He heard Lazarus was sick, He should have dropped everything and come right away. Why stay two extra days? He's in the general vicinity of Bethany, for crying out loud.

It should also be pointed out that the disciples didn't really want to go back to that area. There were Jews in Judea who wanted to stone Jesus. They were perfectly happy staying far, far away from trouble.

When Jesus starts to speak in metaphors about how Lazarus is sleeping, the disciples become really confused. So He has to spell it out for them. (John 11:11-14).

Lazarus is dead.

He follows up with a strange reaction in verse 15: "And for your sakes, I'm glad I wasn't there."

I want you to circle the phrase "for your sakes." Healing His friend two days ago would have been just another miracle. But Jesus knows what is best. He's glad He wasn't there to heal Lazarus immediately. Why?

Because in a few days, everyone will believe. Everyone will trust. They will know His power. They will know and they will believe.

Jesus rallies the troops, turns around, and finally heads for Bethany. He's about to wake the dead guy up. So Thomas said to his fellow disciples, "Let us also go, that we may die with Him" (John 11:16 NIV).

Don't you just love Thomas' attitude? He's like a sullen teenager. "It's going to be disastrous, but let's pack some snacks for the road trip. I call shotgun."

When Jesus asked us to move from one side of Houston to the other side of Houston, like Thomas, I knew it was going to be disastrous. I knew no one would talk to us. I wouldn't have any friends. And their HEB grocery store would never be as good as the other one.

That move has been one of the greatest blessings of our lives.

Let's go, so we may die with Him.

Engage.

How does including God on your list make you feel?

What's the difference between God being good and God being sovereign?

Why do you think Jesus waited so many days before returning to Bethany?

How would that have made you feel if you were Mary or Martha?

Lord, there are countless times I don't understand what Your hand is doing. Build in me a faith that trusts Your heart even when I don't get it. And be near to me in the confusing times and the times that seem hopeless. Remind me what's true: You are in control, You are good, You are present, and You are at work. I want to trust You.

17

Believe.

Continuing with Mary and Martha's story, Lazarus had been dead in the tomb for four days. You know that smell was pungent. Also, where the heck was Jesus?!

Townsfolk had probably seen people come awake or get well after being dead for three days, thanks to sorcerers and other evil forces with power. If Jesus had raised Lazarus after three days, some people might have been skeptical. Jesus' deity would be in question.

Jesus is always intentional. Nothing is by happenstance.

Four days, on the other hand. Yikes. Your back is up against a wall. Call the phone tree and start making the potluck dinner because we've got a funeral to plan. Lazarus just wasn't dead. He was really, really dead.

Many came to the sisters to comfort their grief. Martha heard that Jesus was heading up the driveway, so she ran to meet Him. Mary stayed put. (John 11:19-20).

Martha stands before the Lord and says, "If only You had been here, my brother would not have died" (John 11:21). That's bold, Martha. This is the Messiah you're talking to.

Jesus said to her in John 11:23, "Your brother will rise again." As a good Sunday School student, Martha spouts off that she knows Lazarus will rise again. During the resurrection. But what about now?

Jesus asserts, "I am the resurrection and the life" (John 11:25). He's standing right there in front of Martha. He wants her to connect. He wants her to believe. She is responsible for her decision to follow Him.

Jesus knows that Martha is seeing things in the natural world right now. But He wants her to see that He's giving her His life. Not a belief system. Not a set of rules. Not a culture or a religion. It's His life and He wants to know if she believes.

She says again, "Yes, Lord; I believe that You are the Christ, the Son of God, Who is coming into the world" (John 11:27 ESV). Do you see that she's able to answer and she's able to articulate what is true? But where's her heart?

Shedding light on Mary's heart helps us understand Martha a little bit more.

> Then she returned to Mary. She called Mary aside from the mourners and told her, "The Teacher is here and wants to see you." So Mary immediately went to Him. When Mary arrived and saw Jesus, she fell at His feet and said, "Lord, if only You had been here, my brother would not have died." (John 11:28-29, 32).

This is what I love about the Lord. He does not despise your questions, your doubts or your anger.

Isn't that exactly what Martha said? What's the difference?

They may have said the same thing, but their hearts were in a different posture. It indicates a different level of relationship with Jesus. A different understanding, a different intimacy.

This is what I love about the Lord. He does not despise your questions. He does not despise your doubts. He does not despise your anger.

Scripture states that Jesus loved both Mary and Martha. (John 11:5). We are all His favorites. He shows up every time and He comes in and He stores up our tears. And He holds us like a lamb with a broken leg and He carries us back home to a place of healing.

He's so, so good. He's so tender. And He shows up every time. He is faithful.

"When Jesus saw Mary weeping and the Jews who had come with her were also weeping, He was deeply moved in His spirit and He was greatly troubled" (John 11:33 NIV). He already knew that Lazarus was going to come back. Jesus already knew He was going to raise him from the dead. And yet Mary's broken heart mattered to Him.

In fact, Jesus also wept. (John 11:35).

We live in a broken world. Evil happens. People shoot other people. People abuse other people. People leave other people. People die of disease. And Jesus weeps. And one day is coming where there will be no more tears. But while I run my race, I am not guaranteed that I will not be a casualty. I am not guaranteed that I will not die of cancer. I am not guaranteed that my children will outlive me. I am not guaranteed that tragedy will not befall me.

What am I guaranteed? I am guaranteed Him. He will never leave me or forsake me. (Hebrews 13:5). He holds me in the palm of His hand and no one can snatch me out of it. (John 10:28). And lo, He will be with me until the end of time. (Matthew 28:20).

His guarantee is the same for you.

Reality check: When tragedy does come crashing down around me, I am so bewildered and disappointed because it happened. Understandably so, there's no shame in that. But it becomes one of those low points on my life lines and I get stuck there. And I stay there. And I get mad.

Instead of pressing in like Mary did, I stand with knees locked and vow to self-protect. I choose the safe route. I show up at church because God forbid Sally doesn't see me smiling in that third pew every Sunday morning. What would my friends think if I stopped coming to Bible study?

Jesus loves you. He loves you. You're not disqualified. He's got plans for you. (Jeremiah 29:11). He's going to redeem what was stolen. (Deuteronomy 30:3). He's going to bring beauty from ashes. (Isaiah 61:3). The enemy's doing a number on your mind right now and you are filled with shame. Get right back in the presence of the Lord. He will remind you of what is true.

To think for a minute that Jesus is surprised by our depravity indicates that somehow we think we can pull this thing off. And He's saying, "Look at the cross. Every bit of it. Past sin, present sin, and future sin, all died for on the cross. And the shame that goes with it."

Jesus is going to take the something awful and weave it into a crazy, beautiful tapestry that only He can do.

Will you believe that or not? Jesus is going to take the something awful and weave it into a crazy, beautiful tapestry that only He can do.

And your greatest place of pain will be your greatest place of ministry. You will minister to people that come limping in, that are hemorrhaging, and you're going to empathize because you've been down that road.

You may not have a formula on how to fix it, but you can point them to Jesus.

Now, back to our story.

Jesus is finally ready to raise Lazarus. Hallelujah. He directs someone to take away the stone in front of the tomb and sweet, bless her heart Martha reminds Jesus that it's been four days and there will probably be an odor. (John 11:39).

You know she had a certain tone when she said that, right? A tone that may indicate that it could have been LESS THAN four days if Someone had chosen to come when He was called. Four days is four too many.

> Jesus responded, "Didn't I tell you that you would see God's glory if you believe?" So they rolled the stone aside. Then Jesus looked up to heaven and said, "Father, thank You for hearing me. You always hear me, but I said it out loud for the sake of all these people standing here, so that they will believe You sent me." Then Jesus shouted, "Lazarus, come out!" And the dead man came out, his hands and feet bound in graveclothes, his face wrapped in a headcloth. Jesus told them, "Unwrap him and let him go!" (John 11:40-44).

Everyone who came with Mary and Martha to the tomb saw what Jesus did and they rejoiced. They saw and they believed. (John 11:45).

Here's what I think happened as Lazarus came out the tomb. Martha is beside herself, unwrapping her brother from the linens. There's a celebratory party in the works. And there's Mary, laying at Jesus' feet. Worshiping Him.

Because Jesus was always center stage in her life. Always.

Engage.

Would you have reacted like Martha or like Mary upon seeing Jesus?

Why do you think Jesus wept? Do you ever imagine Him weeping for your wounds?

Do you believe that your greatest pain can be your greatest ministry? If so, how?

Is Jesus center stage in your life? What would it look like for Him to be there?

Lord, thank You for Mary and Martha, women just like me. I want to know You as the God that weeps with me. As I come close to You God, I hold fast to Your promise that You come close to me. (James 4:8). In Your presence Jesus, transform my heart to one that believes You, no matter what.

Finish.

The road to forgiveness is unchartered territory for some of us. Especially when reconciliation enters the picture. We wonder if the relationship can be restored. We question if God commands that we forgive, does He also command that we excuse the person who hurt us so deeply? Does the relationship have to be restored in order for forgiveness to "work"?

The short answer is no.

Remember, forgiveness is an act of obedience between you and the Lord, and you and the Lord only. Reconciliation is His work to complete and it can look a thousand different ways.

The key is allowing the Lord to be the leader in reconciliation.

It will not help me a bit to grab the reins and try and demand the restoration of a certain relationship. I will carry my wounds and the debts to the cross and I will place them there. I surrender it all. Completely. I trust Jesus to restore my soul and the relationships as He sees fit.

I surrender it all. Completely. I trust Jesus to restore my soul and the relationships as He sees fit.

Let's go back to Joseph again. He made some mistakes and most assuredly, his own name was on his list of debts. But he had also been deeply wounded and abused by his own family. Those that should have protected him were the same ones who harmed him. Those wounds changed the trajectory of his life and would have ruined his life had God not been good and sovereign.

And in control of it all.

"But the Lord was with Joseph in the prison and showed him His faithful love" (Genesis 39:21a).

After years of heartbreak and confusion, Joseph probably spent many nights rehearsing his list, fantasizing about all the different things he would do or say to his brothers if he had the chance to see them again.

I suspect item number one on his evil master plan was "locate hole large enough for many brothers." Item two: "Buy new technicolor dreamcoat."

God had a different plan for Joseph. His plan was freedom and purpose.

Several times in Genesis, we see Joseph weeping over the pain and brokenness in his family. I presume he longed for reconciliation, but he didn't spend years focused on the lost relationships with his father and brothers. Instead he fixed his eyes on God and the purpose that lay before him.

The purpose? Serving as the commander of Egypt second only to Pharoah. Joseph interprets a few more dreams and learns that there will be seven years of favor followed by seven years of famine. He prepares Egypt and when the hard times finally hit, many people are able to survive. (Genesis 41).

Including Joseph's brothers.

They don't recognize the man who stands before them. Joseph was a seventeen-year-old supermodel when they sold him into slavery. This man is strong, handsome, and powerful. And he extends grace to his family by offering them food, shelter, and a life in Egypt. (Genesis 42).

At last, the brothers bow down to Joseph, fulfilling the dreamer's prophecy that faithful morning around the breakfast table. (Genesis 42:6b).

Joseph lived his life in step with God, and in due time, God brought reconciliation.

> After burying Jacob, Joseph returned to Egypt with his brothers and all who had accompanied him to his father's burial. But now that their father was dead, Joseph's brothers became fearful. "Now Joseph will show his anger and pay us back for all the wrong we did to him," they said.
>
> So they sent this message to Joseph: "Before your father died, he instructed us to say to you: 'Please forgive your brothers for the great wrong they did to you—for their sin in treating you so cruelly. So we, the servants of the God of your father, beg you to forgive our sin.'" When Joseph received the message, he broke down and wept. Then his brothers came and threw themselves down before Joseph. "Look, we are your slaves!" they said.
>
> But Joseph replied, "Don't be afraid of me. Am I God, that I can punish you? You intended to harm me, but God intended it all for good. He brought me to this position so I could save the lives of many people. No, don't be afraid. I will continue to take care of you and your children." So he reassured them by speaking kindly to them (Genesis 50:14-21).

Had Joseph grabbed control and tried to force something to happen sooner, it would probably have been disastrous. But instead, he trusted God with forgiveness AND reconciliation.

Let's wrap up Mary and Martha's story. At the end of Chapter 17, I talked about how Mary kept Jesus center stage in her life and that made the all difference. How?

Flip over to Luke 10:38-42. In this passage, Martha is busy worrying over a big dinner she was preparing for Jesus. Add to the hostess frenzy, she's highly irritated that she's in the kitchen slaving away over the stove, while her sister sits at Jesus' feet.

Martha is so mad that she tells Jesus to make Mary come help her.

You gotta love Martha. What spunk to boss Jesus around like that! It's killing her to be in earshot of what's happening, but not be a participant.

What happens when I live within earshot? I start to compare. I get really cranky. And I complain that things aren't fair.

Mary, on the other hand, is seated at His feet with the disciples. Do you realize that a woman sitting with the men would not have been culturally acceptable? Add to that, a woman to join the men as a disciple? Unheard of!

Having fellowship and being intimate with the Lord won't always be socially acceptable. But I love that Jesus does not condemn Martha. Jesus is beckoning Martha to more. She doesn't need to be upset over all the details. There really is only one thing worth being concerned about and Mary has discovered it.

Powerful, isn't it?

Fix your eyes on Jesus. Spend time with the Lord. Clear your list. Anticipate that your schedule is going to get busier than ever in the near future. Recognize that you're never going to feel like taking these steps. Count on the fact that you'll come up with ten really good reasons why you should do something different, like watch all ten seasons of Friends on Netflix.

More worthy than the freedom is finding Jesus in the process. His presence is more precious than any answered prayer. He is always worth it.

I want you to decide today that you're going to finish the race. Specifically, you're going to do the work of forgiveness because otherwise, you're just going to run with a limp.

Trust Him enough to go through the difficulty or the pain of forgiveness, of clearing your list, so that you can run freely.

Trust Him enough to know that there is freedom on the other side and that freedom is for you.

More worthy than the freedom is finding Jesus in the process. His presence is more precious than any answered prayer. He is always worth it.

Jesus, You are worth it all. All the pain. All the time. All the energy. Because only You bring beauty from ashes. Only You can restore what's been lost. Only You. It's always, only You. I love You.

Notes.

Whether reflecting by yourself or exploring with a small group, *Forgive. Freedom Is Worth It* is meant to encourage your work of forgiveness. This section cites sources and also provides a topical scripture resource for you to draw closer in to the powerful truths found between these covers. Organized by chapter, the topics are pulled straight out of the text or prayers and are followed by a page reference to easily find the context.

Grab a journal. Open your Bible. We invite you to discover the freedom God has in store for you.

Start.

He demonstrates forgiveness over and over. (page 15)

Isaiah 55:7

Micah 7:18

1 John 1:9

We are Your beloved children. (page 16)

Ephesians 5:1

1 John 3:2

1
Favored.

Life of Joseph (page 17)

Genesis 30-50

You are my helper and I will have no fear. (page 22)

Exodus 15:2

Psalm 18:2

Psalm 40:17

Psalm 46:1-2

Psalm 54:4

Psalm 62:6

Psalm 70:5

Psalm 118:6

Isaiah 50:9

Hebrews 13:6

[1]Søren Kierkegaard, *Journalen JJ:167 (1843), Søren Kierkegaards Skrifter*, (Copenhagen: Søren Kierkegaard Research Center, 1997), volume 18, 306.

2
Stuck.

You delight in us and long to sing over us. (page 29)

Psalm 37:23

Zephaniah 3:17

3
Tangled.

Fix your eyes on Jesus. (page 33)

Psalm 46:10

Psalm 57:7

Jeremiah 29:13

John 17:3

Philippians 3:13-14

Colossians 3:1

Hebrews 12:2

You are God that frees me. (page 37)

Isaiah 61:1

Matthew 1:21

Luke 4:18

John 8:32-36

Romans 6:22-23

Romans 8:1-2

2 Corinthians 3:17

[2]Luke Kerr-Dineen, "23 Inspiring Quotes from Coach Eric Taylor that Prove He's the Best," *USA Today,* March, 17, 2017, accessed August 10, 2018, https://ftw.usatoday.com/2017/03/best-friday-night-lights-quotes-coach-eric-taylor.

4
Wounded.

The wages of sin is death. (page 44)

Romans 6:23

Galatians 3:13

You love me. (page 46)

John 3:16

John 15:12-13

Romans 5:8

Romans 8:37-39

Ephesians 2:4-5

5
Messy.

Jesus is the pure, spotless Lamb of God. ***(page 49)***

Isaiah 53:7

John 1:29

1 Peter 1:19

Revelation 5:12-14

Revelation 12:11

Grace is free, but it cost Jesus everything. ***(page 50)***

Acts 15:11

Romans 5:15

Ephesians 1:6-7

Ephesians 2:8

Jesus' blood covers your sin. ***(page 50)***

Acts 20:28

Romans 3:24-25

Romans 5:9

Ephesians 1:7

Ephesians 2:13

Colossians 1:20

Hebrews 9:14

Hebrews 9:22

1 Peter 1:18-19

1 John 1:7

6
Sidelined.

Jesus removed the shame. ***(page 54)***

Isaiah 54:4

Romans 5:3-5

Romans 10:11
Hebrews 12:2
1 Peter 2:6

He has called you by name. (page 55)
Deuteronomy 28:10
Isaiah 43:1
Jeremiah 14:9
Jeremiah 15:16

7
Indebted.

Jesus commands that we forgive. (page 61)
Matthew 18:21-22
Luke 6:37
Ephesians 4:32

[3]"Forgiveness: Your Health Depends on It," *Healthy Connections*, https://www.hopkinsmedicine.org/health/healthy_aging/healthy_connections/forgiveness-your-health-depends-on-it.

[4]Lewis B. Smedes, *FORGIVE AND FORGET: Healing the Hurts We Don't Deserve* (New York: HarperCollins Publishers, 1984), 79.

[5]"Max Lucado Quotes," *Good Reads*, https://www.goodreads.com/quotes/45952.

8
List.

David cries out to the Lord. (page 73)

Psalm 13

Psalm 18

Psalm 40:1

Psalm 54

Psalm 55

Psalm 69

Psalm 86

Psalm 141

You are my refuge in whom I trust. (page 75)

2 Samuel 22:3

Psalm 18:2

Psalm 62:7

Psalm 73:28

Psalm 91:2

Psalm 94:22

Psalm 144:2

[6]"The Meaning of Marriage: Facing the Complexities of Commitment with the Wisdom of God by Timothy J. Keller," *Good Reads*, https://www.goodreads.com/work/quotes/16321346.

9
Steps.

You are the Great Healer. (page 79)

Exodus 15:26

Psalm 41:3

Psalm 147:3

Proverbs 3:5-8

[7]"Guideposts Classics: Corrie ten Boom on Forgiveness," *Guideposts*, last modified July 24,2014, https://secure.guideposts.org/better-living/guideposts-classics-corrie-ten-boom-on-forgiveness.

[8]Hamilton Smith, *Extracts from the Writings of Thomas Watson (London, The Central Bible Truth Depot, 1915), 73, https://books.google.com.*

10
Tell.

Give all your worries and cares to Him. (page 82)

Psalm 55:22
Proverbs 3:5-6
Matthew 6:25-34
Matthew 11:28-30
Philippians 4:6-7
1 Peter 5:6-7

Your perfect love will drive out my fear. (page 83)

Psalm 23:4
Psalm 56:3
Isaiah 41:13
John 14:27
Hebrews 13:5-6
1 John 4:18

Your steadfast presence will be my courage. (page 83)

Deuteronomy 31:6
Joshua 1:9
1 Chronicles 28:20
Psalm 16:11
Psalm 23:1-4
Psalm 27:1
Lamentations 3:22-24

John 16:33
Ephesians 6:10
2 Thessalonians 3:5

11
Feel.

Life of David (page 87)
1 Samuel 16-30
2 Samuel
1 Kings 1-2:12
1 Chronicles 28-29

Your Word promises me that I am not alone. (page 88)
Joshua 1:5
Joshua 1:9
Matthew 28:20
John 16:32

12
Cancel.

Sins have consequences. (page 91)
Proverbs 28:13
Isaiah 59:2
Ezekiel 18:20
Romans 5:12
Galatians 6:7-8

I will send the Spirit of truth. (page 92)

John 14:16-17

John 15:26

John 16:13

1 John 4:6

13
Accept.

You stand in the gap and supply my every need. (page 95)

Luke 22:32

Luke 23:34

Romans 8:34

Phillipians 4:19

Hebrews 7:24-25

1 John 2:1

[9]Smedes, *FORGIVE AND FORGET,* 29.

14
Risk.

Teach me to wait on the Lord. (page 98)

Genesis 49:18

Psalm 25:5

Psalm 27:14

Psalm 33:20

Psalm 37:7

Psalm 130:5

Isaiah 30:18

Isaiah 40:31

Lamentations 3:24-26

Hosea 12:6

Micah 7:7
Romans 8:23
Galatians 5:5
Hebrews 9:28
James 5:7-8

You are the God of reconciliation. (page 98)
2 Corinthians 5:18-19
Colossians 1:20

God is a redeeming God. (page 99)
Exodus 6:6
Isaiah 44:22
Romans 3:23-25
Galatians 3:13
Galatians 4:4-5
Ephesians 1:7
Colossians 1:13-14
Titus 2:14

15
Question.

The questions David asked when hurting. (page 103)
Psalm 6:3
Psalm 8:4
Psalm 10:1
Psalm 13:1-2
Psalm 15:1
Psalm 22:1-2
Psalm 27:1
Psalm 42:9
Psalm 44:24
Psalm 74:1
Psalm 74:10

16
Trust.

Life of Mary/Martha/Lazarus (page 109)

Matthew 26:6-13

Mark 14:3-9

Luke 10:38-42

John 11:1-45

John 12:1-11

Jesus says we should pray and ask for healing. (page 110)

Jeremiah 30:17

Jeremiah 33:6

James 5:14-16

17
Believe.

I am guaranteed Him. (page 117)

1 Corinthians 15:20-23

2 Corinthians 1:20-22

2 Corinthians 5:5

Ephesians 1:13-14

Hebrews 7:20-28

Finish.

Joseph weeps over the pain and brokenness in his family. (page 122)

Genesis 42:24

Genesis 43:30

Genesis 45:2

Genesis 50:17

Laura.

Laura Seifert was working in corporate America when she felt God calling her to leave her corner office for a ministry job in a trailer (seriously). She has been involved in ministry for more than twenty years, serving in various roles, but has always loved working with women the most. She has a passion for teaching women and helping them access the profound truths of God's Word.

In 2000, Laura became a licensed minister of the gospel and in 2016, she founded Yes. ministries. Laura and the Yes. team host Bible studies, events, and retreats to help draw all women closer to Jesus by saying YES to God's promises in Christ and trusting Him during the unknown.

Laura is a graduate of Texas A&M University and is minorly obsessed with finding a good pair of jeans on sale. But most of all, she loves being the mother to kids Ben and Beth and dog Jesse. Together with her wonderful husband and pastor Jason, the Seiferts call Friendswood, Texas, home.

Resources.

To order more copies of
Forgive. Freedom Is Worth It, go to
www.yesministries.net/forgive

To hear Laura's podcasts
or inquire about speaking engagements, go to
www.yesministries.net

Yes. ministries exists to draw all women closer to Jesus.

The Yes to all of God's promises is in Christ, and through Christ we say Yes to the glory of God.
2 Corinthians 1:20.

Yes. ministries, based in Houston, Texas, and founded by Laura Seifert, hosts Bible studies, events and retreats throughout the year to help women engage in God's word.

Yes. ministries is about saying "yes" to God in obedience and trusting him in the unknown. We want to celebrate and share women's stories of faith in an effort to encourage others to say "yes" to God. Our vision and hope is that these stories of faith would be a great reminder to women of the power of God and that through them women across the world would draw closer to Jesus.

To find our events, access Laura's podcast, request Laura to speak at your event, submit a prayer request, share your Yes Story or just say hi, check out our website at

www.yesministries.net

We look forward to meeting you!

Yes. ministries is a 501(c)(3) organization.